Dedication

This book is dedicated to all those who had to experience painfully what war in a foreign land means and those at home who did not know what the soldiers had to face in the field.

In particular, I dedicate the book to my son Marco, who had to make do without a lot as a little boy because of my absence. In his mind he was with me all the time.

In memory of all comrades who have fallen in action, in particular:

Sergeant Christian S., Panzer Grenadier Battalion 332, fallen in an attack at Rustak on 25. June 2005 and

Lieutenant Colonel Armin-Harry F., Reservist, who fell in a suicide attack in Kabul on 14. November 2005.

Andreas Meyer

YOU COULD DIE ANY DAY

BEING DEPLOYED TO AFGHANISTAN AS A SOLDIER OF THE GERMAN ARMY.

 tredition®

Publisher: tredition GmbH, Halenreie 40-44
        22359 Hamburg Germany

ISBN
Paperback   ISBN: 978-3-347-09331-7
Hardcover   ISBN: 978-3-347-09332-4
eBook   ISBN: 978-3-347-09333-1

Bibliographic information of the German National Library:

The German National Library records this publication in the German National Bibliographic; detailed bibliographic information is provided via the following link: http://dnb.ddb.de

Contents list

Prologue...13

1 January 2005..15

2. Preparations..20

3. March 2005 24

4. June 2005, Mission......................................30

5. Every day camp life.....................................38

6. Support from Austria...................................45

7. A baker and his flatbread 50

8. At the medic`s...51

9. Earthquake in Pakistan 55

10. My time in between the missions 62

11. Second deployment.....................................64

12. The next flight to Afganistan 66

13. Preparation for handover 73

14. Challenges at the IEB-Cell........................76

15. Visit tot he police chief at the airport...........80

16. First tasks fort he new unit......................84

17. Charity for a orphanage.............................90

18. Meeting again after 13 years......................95

19. The Blue Moque of Mazar-E-Sharif..............98

20. Visit by the commander 103

21. Driving to the Teacher Training Center.......105

22. Religious dignitaries at Camp Marmal......108

23. The newbies are coming 111

24. Getting acquainted with medical personal during flight 114

25. A day in the camp with five students.........116

26. Afghanistan-Projekt „no más fonteras".......122

27. US-American artist arrives............................125

28. The great day oft he experiment has come .135

29. Trip tot he border and port city Hairatan ...141

30. First visit tot he OCCR headqzarters...........145

31. Viait oft he Gouvernor of Samangan 150

32. The first watch on the watch tower..............155

33. Support in driving service for OCCR..........160

34. Mr. Scholl-Latour visits Camp Marmal 161

35. My third mission 165

36. And back again in Mazar-e Sharif 168

37. After 16 days camp stay...................................173

38. The first days in office as troop supply officer 176

39. Support fort he engineer squad....................178

40. Evening remembrance service for four fallen comrades..182

41. The blue heart of Feyzabad 186

42. Lunch with „Schoko"..190

43. A reunion with Nabil, Sultan, Soraya 194

44. Attack on German armed forces in Takhar province 196

45. Father`s Day run at Camp Feyzabad............200

46. Departure 205

47. Back home 208

48. Eqilogue..211

49. Attachment 1 Rank groups from army 214

50. Attachment 2 Mongolian ranks 215

51. Attachment 3 Breakdown of a guide 216

52. Attachment 4 Classification of NATO classes 217

53. Attachment 4 Translation from German to Dari...218

54. Attachment 5 in alphabetic order 220

55. Attachment 6 List of figures 225

Thanks to:

F or the patient support in the implementation of this book, I thank my friend Jana Wochnik-Sachtleben, who has lectured the text, and recorded my audio book, as well as Ms. Miriam Hadji for the design of the impressive book cover, and the translators Maren Krüger, Kerry S and Alexander Langer.
I warmly thank my comrade and friend Nabil Azizi for the translation into Dari language.

I also especially thank my partner, "Thessi", for her constant support the whole time.
 I would also like to thank the following former senior officers and civilians as well as all my former comrades who dealt with me directly and indirectly in the missions:
 Brigadier A., Airborne Brigade 25,
Colonel B., former company commander paratrooper battalion 253, Nagold,
Brigadier General R., former commander of the Center for Operational Information in Mayen,
Peter Scholl-Latour, German-French journalist and publicist from Bad Honnef,
Batuz, an American artist, philosopher and cultural activist,
and my closest comrades in the time of the missions (2005, 2010, 2011), Rainer M., Thomas K., Tino M., Marcel G., Soraya A., Sultan A., Nabil A., Alexander B., Marc -Andre S., Tobias M., Stephan M., Christian W.

Pretext:

These words are mine, a report from a staff sergeant of the reserve, who retired from active service in the German Army in 1990, but after a six-year break decided to live a life in uniform again and volunteered as a reservist for three missions in Afghanistan.

Previously, I had been soldier for eight years, but what I had learned those days was nothing to put into practice at that time, because back then there was no mandate for foreign missions for the Bundeswehr.

Then, after the attacks on the World Trade Center in New York, USA, on September 11, 2001, the circumstances changed.

From this point on, the Bundeswehr also participated in the foreign missions of the NATO troops. In December 2014, the ISAF mission ended in Afghanistan and a new advisory and training mission began.

During the period from 2001 to the end of 2014, a total of 3,687 soldiers, including 54 German soldiers, lost their lives. All were comrades, some of them were my friends.

This is my - and their - story.

Prologue

September 11 2001 I sat at a desk of a logistics company I was employed at as fire warden and coordinator for medical assistance since I left the Bundeswehr from active duty. I was responsible for the preventive fire security and all related aspects within the company. I liked my job. Being the one responsible for the security of my colleagues and having the possibility to be proactive always gave me a good feeling. Since I am a challenge loving person I was really satisfied with my tasks.

This morning though, my whole well settled life was about change in a dramatic way. A change that effected many more people around the globe.

A colleague of mine shouted over to me, I should open the website of CNN. Something about a plane had hit a sky scraper. Moments later I was following the live broadcast from the accident site staring at the horrific inferno of what once used to be the World Trade Center. I could not beliving my own eyes when the second jet flew into the other tower of the WTC.

In the first moment everything looked so staged. Like it was just not real. Like a really really bad movie. But it was real. And the consequences of this new reality were about to affect not only the world in general but also my very own personal life. I was about to face the terror from eye to eye. Not in the states but in Afghanistan.

I rejoined the Bundeswehr and became a soldier once again.

Map of Afghanistan

1 January 2005

10th of January 2005 I received a call from the company sergeant ("Spieß") of my former unit, the 294th Mechanized Infantry Brigade. He was looking for a logistics assistant for the upcoming overseas mission. The destination: KUNDUZ, Afghanistan. I was quite surprised. But being a member of the reserve with still valid certification for this kind of position I had no doubt that I was going to support and accompany any battalion they would assign me to. At that time, I had a good job. I had responsibilities. But nothing could stop me from going with them. It´s one of these things you become a soldier for. Yes, of course I had been in the Army for 8 long years already. But it was nothing compared to what was about to come. Those years we´ve only been to countless exercises. All with the same scenarios. All about the same enemy. The enemy those days: "The East". In that past, counterterrorism and asymmetric warfare, at least in Germany, were not even close to become a term the army would focus on. You had 2 nations or blocks in conflict. Blue and red. Blue = good. Red = evil. After 9/11 the whole role of the Bundeswehr and its enemies had changed rapidly.

After the phone conversation with my "Spieß" I went straight to my boss asking him for approval to join the Bundeswehr for active duty to go on mission. He was far away from being amazed by my idea, but after a long discussion about a man´s values and appealing to his idealism he finally agreed. After taking care of all administrative things with my employer and covering all needed aspects with my family I confirmed my participation in the upcoming mission. The preparations for my first mission began.

Those days I felt like I would finally do something meaningful for those people who had known only three things in the last year: war, suffering and oppression, caused by the same inhuman creatures who attacked the way of life of the western world. There are so many thoughts running through your head while preparing for a mission. You need some time to get their true meaning. To realize what is coming up to you. I was married at that time and my son had just turned 7. It was a hard battle to convince my wife. But like many times before my will won over her concerns.

During the time of my active duty in the past I learned the true meaning of comradeship. What it means to have true fellow soldiers. This understanding already began with my first day in basic training. 12 completely different characters put into a tiny room in a lousy barrack forced to come along with each other for months. Back then, a lot of the guys were away from home for the very first time in their life which led to the funny picture of a crazy long cue in front of the only phone cell on our military base every single evening. Fortunately, I was spared that kind of homesickness since I had left my home early to be trained as a cook prior to joining the military. But these new dogmas of order and obedience left a strange taste inside my mouth and stomach.

Coming back to camaraderie, I witnessed that we were capable of achieving anything as long we stood together. Within the group as well as with the platoon. You help each other no matter what. Being it the seemingly endless marches, the combat and survival exercises or our final military exam. You carry the backpack of someone who is close to collapse. You turn around and grab a guy whose legs refuse to keep on running. You do all this because you can be sure that they would do all this for you as well once you faced your limits. It was a uniquely good feeling to know this each time we managed an exercise or task. This feeling stayed throughout all my courses and later in the everyday military life. The things I learned and the role models I was led by created the credo I used through my military career as a Sergeant leading young people myself. "I, as a sqad leader won´t expect or force anyone to do anything that I am not capable of doing myself." Just like Alexandre Dumas wrote in "The three musketeers" One for all and all for one! Those years in the army really brought me forward as a human being in many aspects.

In Germany of the 1980s the relationship between the civilian population and its countries' forces and the picture the people had of its soldiers was a much better one than nowadays. You could see it specially during the large exercises like 1984 "Flinker Igel" or 1987 "Kecker Spatz". Farmers would let you rest and sleep in their barn and when you had to make a tactical stop in front of a gymnasium of a school, kids would gather around and watch you curiously. Often, people would bring you fresh bread, eggs, bacon and refreshments. Sometimes civilians were even directly involved in the exercise by helping out or give a hand to set up our infrastructure. As the field cook, I always had more than enough work to do. Being responsible for the food supply kept me busy every single minute, especially when I had to care about groups being deployed on very short notice.

In these cases, I was happy to have my little helpers around. Meaning, whenever we had a bunch of guys having to deploy within minutes I just placed crates with the different goods on cued tables, positioned my helpers behind the crates and let them pack the food packages, then passing them on to the next helper in the chain like in a little factory.

These little helpers were kids from the nearby villages who were always happy to be a part in this.

Remembering this time as a young Sergeant and field cook, there is another episode coming to my mind which was positive as well and which should convince me one more time of how small the world is. I was preparing the dough for an apple pie that was planned as a special treat for the next morning´s breakfast for the company when a high-ranking officer suddenly opened the door and appeared right in front of me. Normally you would jump into attention immediately and do a military salute but I was kind of confused by this surprising visit. I guess that was obvious to him and with an expression in his eyes that I have never forgot since then he just said: "no report needed soldier.

What tasty treat is it you have there? " And with these words he came closer and put his finger right into the dough. I was just saying: "So what do you think?" He just laughed and said that it is a shame that he won´t be there to try it tomorrow morning because he loves apple pie so much. I almost .... in my pants. I had never met such a high-ranking officer before and this guy was a Colonel. This Colonel, this episode of camaraderie made a very strong impression on me although I had no clue who he was. Years later we met again. Not in Germany but in Afghanistan. That time I of course knew who he was. Brigade General and Commander of the 8th German mission contingent to ISAF, General A.

During the time of my first enlistment to the army I came to know another very impressive man, Colonel B. Back then he was a Major and became my company commander in NAGOLD in 1987. Later, after 41 years of service, he served as the commander of the airborne and air transportation school in ALTENSTADT. These 2 men had a very strong influence on me and my military career through all the years which I am very grateful for.

2. Preparations

The preparations for my very first deployment began with the standard medical checks and countless vaccinations. Tetanus, Hepatitis A and B, rabies and so on...I got it all. All was documented meticulously via a timeline checklist according to an individually specified vaccination scheme for the deployment region. There is a scheme for every different region.

Once I got the approval by the medics I was sent on the mission specified basics training (ESGA) in STETTEN AM KALTEN MARKT followed by the centralized combat troops training (ZENTRA) in HAMMELBURG at the Training Centre of Infantry. The training was very accurate. From mine and improvised explosives device (IED) detection to a very realistic scenario of being captured and held hostage, we trained every possible situation we could get into during the mission. Another important part of the training was the cultural education with insights into afghan population, habits and social structure as well as a basics language training of the most important phrases. We got a bunch of handbooks and vocabularies German - Paschtu and German - Dari, the two main languages that are officially used in Afghanistan.

There is a picture in one of the handbooks showing an Afghan building an IED made of fertilizer. That one remained in my mind till today. He was using a yellow canister. The officer who conducted the lesson told us to always pay attention to these canisters if we see them. A nice advise that some time later unfortunately showed to be absolutely useless, but we will return to this topic.

After the described preparation training followed the preparation for the individual tasks in the battalion (BN) in the ALBKASERNE in STETTEN. Lots of meetings and briefings with the Chief of logistics (J4 officer) and the BN commander were to be hold. Everything related to personnel and material was planned to the smallest detail. That time I also had to join all kind of individual mission task related trainings like Peace Support Operations PSO or workshops for logistics personnel and specialists of the Mission Contingent of the ISAF mission.

In advance of the actual deployment I additionally had to join a reconnaissance mission to AFG to the place of our responsibility at the Provincial Reconstruction Team (PRT) at KUNDUZ. Our team consisted of 4 officers and 2 sergeants including me, who were given the task to evaluate the situation on ground in and around the operational base and to verify the information we had received till then. Although we were provided with quite a lot of data we wanted to be sure that they were still up to date and reliable. Next time I would arrive here as the BNs TVB responsible for the supply and provision of our soldiers, not only in the camp and nearby areas, but also for the ones on missions and at the forward operation bases (FOB) deep in enemy territory. This is completely different from doing this job back home. In mission country you cannot just drive over to the next garage to get spare parts for your combat vehicle. No, in combat areas the lines of supply are much more complicated and way longer.

sunset in the Camp

Structure wise, I was assigned to the Staff and Supply Company. Due to that I also was responsible for the support with personnel and material of the Staff with its 7 sections as well as the Base Security / Defense Company and the military police. One who has never been in the Bundeswehr may imagine the SSCOY as a huge company with its different departments. In our case for example , there was a canteen with its responsibilities, the "Nachschubzug", which is a supply platoon taking care of pickup and transportation of the supplies arriving at the airport, the "Materialgruppe", a supply group distributing all material and ordering or sending spare parts and damaged parts from and to Germany, the "Instandsetzungsgruppe", mechanics responsible to keep all vehicles operational and the "Luftumschlagszug", an air logistics platoon offloading air transportation and taking care of distributing the mail and material to the areas of operation. As you see there was a lot of personnel and effort needed to keep this machine PRT KUNDUZ running.

3. March 2005

On the 15th of March we started at 12:30 from the military section of the airport of Cologne/Bonn in an Airbus of the Luftwaffe (German Airforce) to our layover in Termez, Uzbekistan (ترمز/اوزبيكستان).

At 21:30 we landed on its airport. Whoever thought he could finally get off the plane was immediately disappointed. The door opened and an Usbek official came in. Accompanied by one of the German Airforce ground crew guys he collected all our military IDs, saying this was a regular procedure to check if the incoming personnel matches with the reported list and that we would get our IDs back when we proceed to our flight on the following morning. One of the guys being deployed for the second time turned over to me, smiled and said that they going to copy them now and forward the data to the Russians. I laughed and said:

"You´re joking, right?"

He laughed back and said:

"No!"

Actually, that was a well-known fact.

Once they had all our IDs, we were allowed to leave the plane and walk over to the so called transit camp which was located only 200 meters away from the runway. It was dark and humid. We were led to the tent area where we could buy a Coke and a more or less warm sausage for dinner. Then we went to our declared tents. Thank god they had air-conditioning, so that we were able to get some rest for at least a few hours. According to local time it was 0100 when we laid down. So it was a short night, because at 0430 we had already boarded again, this time a C-160 Transall on a direct flight to KUNDUZ (كندوز). We had to start that early because later in the morning the temperatures would rise to an unbearable degree. Too hot for the Airforce to fly.

It is 0500 local afghan time at KUNDUZ airport or what those people call to be an airport. The main building was a ruin and the tower looked everything but stable. The first thing drawing my attention were the rays of sun right above the tower and the remains of two destroyed combat helicopters left by the Russians when they withdrew 1989.

We were picked up with some jeeps and Mungos (an ugly tiny military transportation vehicle which was actually concepted as a street cleaning vehicle) and brought to the main base. My first impressions of the country were overwhelming. I sat next to the driver of the Mungo and watched how the life in and around KUNDUZ began the day.

Then suddenly I was hit by a negative feeling. I saw all those children with their small barrows carrying those yellow canisters. Immediately the words of that officer came to my mind when he warned us about these canisters. Could these little children really be assassins? Those with their yellow canisters? But not only they had those canisters. There were yellow canisters everywhere! In each corner. In front of every store. Beside every single road.

The next thing I recognized where all those children working on the fields along the road. Considering that awful crazy heat it was hard to watch. Later I found out that almost all children have to get up very early in the morning to work on the fields together with their parents. Afterwards they go to school and return to the fields in the evening to work again. Like in Germany back then children had to help their parents with their work to assure the families survival, but nowadays this would be far from every imagination. Over here it is still everyday life.

The PRT at the northern afghan provincial capital KUNDUZ was founded by the US forces and was taken over by the Bundeswehr in October 2003. The official tasks of the german-run PRT were:

Support of the official structures of the central afghan government in the provinces of KUNDUZ and TAKHAR in all kinds of aspects.

Different from the time when the PRT was led by the US forces there were also civil officials from Germany present, such as the ministry of foreign affairs, the ministry of interior as well as the ministry of economical cooperation and development who worked very close together with the German military. The camp was guarded and secured by afghan security forces.

Arriving at the camp we were met by our predecessors at the so-called market, which is the central place of the camp and then brought to our quarters where we would stay for the next eight days of our introduction.

The next morning we placed our luggage, which actually consisted only of our combat back pack, on the field beds and went for breakfast. In front of the canteen tent there was a hand washing installation. Hygiene was elementary in the camp. In a country with almost no sanitary infrastructure, the dust of feces is permanently present in the air. At noon it was the worst. No one who was not deployed there can even imagine the smell. A good protection those days was the Kufiya, the typical head scarf which I used to spray with orange perfume and wrapped it around my mouth and nose to avoid breathing in that sickening feces dust. Of course, you were not 100 percent save using this but it helped to make it through the day.

Afghan security forces at work

Entering the canteen, we were just amazed by the variety of all the tasty looking foods that were on offer. It was even more and so much better than in the facilities back home! Fresh fruits, fresh baked bread, cheese, ham, scrambled eggs and even freshly brewed coffee. After having breakfast, the COY commander showed us the most important stations in the camp such as the location of the sections J1 to J6 of which J6 for example was responsible for the whole IT infrastructure of the camp and its forces. After that we visited the security COY. Later that day I got to meet with a SGT 1st class of the COY. His name was Christian S. and his task was to show us around and teach us about the way of life in the camp. We got along with each other quite well from the very first day and spend a lot of time together during my stay.

The following days passed by fast, filled with talks and briefings with leading personnel and endless reports and evaluations. Especially the procedures of ordering and distributing of material, the supply chains and the detailed capacities of the air delivery had our main focus due to the intention to bring in much more material from Germany. Time just flew by and on the last evening before heading back home Christian and me went to the moral welfare (MW) tent to have a drink and some last words until we meet again on the 27th of June for the start of my actual mission deployment. The next morning we said goodbye at the airport where my team and I entered an CH-53 transport helicopter who brought us to TERMEZ and from where we flew back to Cologne.

flight to termez with the CH-53 helicopter

4. June 2005, Mission

I n the company there was still quite some work to be done before my deployment. My additional duties were delegated to the chosen personnel that had to replace me. There was the upcoming inspection of all first aid kits as well as the checking of all defibrillators which had to be ensured while I was gone.

Normally a soldier gets about a week off before the deployment to spend time with his family and loved ones. A so called "cuddle week". In my case it was a little bit different. Even in that particular week I had to work in the company and didn´t have time off to take care of my family like all my fellow soldiers. Of course, we used the evenings after work to spend some time together. At the end my son helped me with packing my deployment box that had to be filled with all the military stuff as well as all the private things like pictures and books. As a guy from the reserve I was lucky to be allowed to fly with all my luggage, in contrast to the regular soldiers who had their additional belongings shipped weeks in advance. Their luggage was collected and flown in with mixed material and personnel air transportation mostly by Luftwaffe assets to the air logistics point in TERMEZ, Uzbekistan. From there the luggage was flown to the mission location by our C-160 Transall; the workhorse of the German Airforce. Heavier loads were flown in by chartered Ukrainian jets like the

Ilyshin IL-76 or even with Antonov AN-124 which is the world`s largest cargo plane.

The time to deploy came closer incredibly fast with every day. This time we were departing not from Cologne but from Frankfurt because most of the soldiers of the 8th german mission contingent were from the south of Germany. My wife and my son accompanied me to the airport and stayed with me until I had to check in. Regardless of our farewell we all were in a good mood although we knew that we will not see each other for more than 4 months. Marco, being 7 years old that time, liked being around so many soldiers in their cool uniforms. Amazed by the moment he was more than happy to pose for photos with me and other soldiers. He played and ran around with my very close comrades Thomas K. and Rainer M. who would be my supporting staff in the J4 environment.

It was a strange feeling to leave my family all alone. The next months I´d be far away and wouldn´t be able to be there for them. But due to the new impressions and experiences the life back home shifted to the back row. The mission became our primary focus. Then in the nights the thoughts about my loved ones came back to my mind and left me sleepless for quite some time. Despite all the risks and danger, I chose the mission because I considered it to be my holy duty for my country to help a threatened land and especially its people. I don´t know if my comrades felt the same way or different those days.

Shortly before the check-in I said goodbye to my wife and son. Until that moment everything felt as if I was just about to go on a vacation with my pals which I actually never did before. Which is weird somehow...I didn´t have the impression that I was going on a mission and that there might be the possibility of never coming back.

I brought my duffel bag and my box to the counter to have it checked in. The friendly guy from the ground crew offered me a nice seat in the jet and gave me my ticket. From the windows of the waiting room you could see to the runway. It was pouring with rain outside but that didn´t bother us at all.

Then it was time. The boarding began. We all drove with a shuttle bus directly to the plane. In the Airbus I sat down and immediately stretched out my legs to check if would feel comfortable with my long legs. Being 1,95 meters tall can become quite a torture on a long flight. On that seat it felt just great. The ground crew guy kept his word. When I looked out of the window it was still raining. At the same moment, over there in KUNDUZ it must be 45 degree in the shade, I thought to myself. I couldn´t stop thinking of it: Tomorrow I´ll be back there. Tomorrow I will meet Thomas in the evening and we will talk about our day and we will play "Kicker" (table football).

Finally, after all these preparations, courses and trainings we were heading to Afghanistan. I get comfortable in my seat and watch the jet filling with people. The boarding is finished quickly and the doors are closed. The Airbus rolls slowly down the runway to its starting point. I feel how the noise inside calms down. All are in their seats. I put on my headphones to listen to music. Some take pictures with their mobile phones or cameras. Everybody is relaxed. We take off on time. Next stop is Nürnberg, where we will pick up the rest of our mixed unit. This doesn´t take longer than an hour and we´re on our way again directly to Termez.

What I didn´t know that moment is that my friend and comrade Oberfeldwebel Christian S. was going to die on this day in a tragic accident. It happened while I was sitting on my flight passing over Russia´s wide country highlighted by beautiful sunshine. No one thought that two comrades would die on such a lovely day. We were landing in Termez at 2230. To make it through the few hours we had to wait for our following flight to Kunduz we were given some tea, some warm sausages and a field bed.

The next morning, we entered the Transall which departed at 0400 to bring us to our final destination. It was still dark when we took off but already an hour later we dashed down almost vertical in a 90 degree angle towards the airport of Kunduz. You need to know that the German pilots in Afghanistan have to fly relaying only on vision, map and compass due to the lack of a more modern aircraft than the C-160. These kinds of maneuvers were absolutely common these days. So everybody was literally thrown out of sleep and seat.

After the landing the sun was shining and the heat was almost killing us. A feeling as if you got hit by a wooden plank right in your face.

I am back in Kunduz. Like six weeks ago we got picked up by Mungos and various jeeps of different brands. Later I asked myself how it is possible to fall in love with a country that you don´t even know. But this country enchants me in a way that I cannot resist. Its people, the surroundings, the exotic smell on its markets and even this awful heat is a mixture to which I got addicted to very fast. It´s like someone flips the switch and the light turns on. Also, the kindness of these people and their hospitality impresses me over and over again.

Arriving at the camp we were welcomed at the "Market" but different from how it was the last time.

The Spieß and the COY commander of our predecessors led us to our provisional accommodations. It´s common that you stay in tents until your predecessors have left. Only then you can move to a solid accommodation. Later that day we picked up our luggage from the air logistics platoon which is located at the other end of the camp.

The camp is located on a big former fruit plantation. On its grounds we have trees with different kinds of fruits like lemon, oranges and figs irrigated by moats running through the whole camp. If you could ignore the hostile environment in the area around us it might feel like holidays. Together with some comrades I brought my bags and the box to my tent where I would stay for the next 14 days. Then it was time for breakfast followed by the standard official welcome of the "new guys".

Due to the short night and the long flight the day before I didn´t think a lot about my arrival. The only thought I perceived for a moment were all those flags that are hoisted on half-mast. But I was too confused by then to recognize its meaning and become upset. In my mind I was already engrossed in my in processing, a procedure every new arrival has to go through. You get a bunch of papers that have to be handed over, signed, stamped or signed by every station to receive your bullet proof west or so called bristol, your pistol, assault rifle and cleaning kit, your bed linen and all the other stuff a soldier needs. This mind grinding and annoying procedure takes you a minimum of 2 to 3 days depending on where the location of each station is at and how quickly you can get there. Of course, you also have to go through the medical check to assure that every necessary medical treatment was done back in Germany.

Later that day I had some unscheduled time, so I went over to the security COY to check if Christian might be in. I entered the tent and asked the first guy I saw if he had an idea of where Christian might be. This front office soldier looked at me kind of confused and pointed to a framed picture with a black ribbon on its left corner that showed Christian. In that moment I was just thinking: " Is that guy f*cking kidding me?!" That must be the worst joke ever. But that private just nodded and explained to me how Christian was killed 2 days ago in an accident with an ammunition truck in the vicinity of Rustack.

I am dumbfounded - I can´t feel anything - emptiness. I can´t believe it. How can Christian be gone? No talks, no hanging around at the MWR tent after duty having drinks or just watch the afghan heaven with all its stars at night and listen to the cicadas? All this should be over now?

Everybody of the new ones were shocked when hearing this tragic news. To stay at good state of mental health everyone of us had to find away cope with such a loss. I have to keep focused on my mission. For that reason, I suppressed my feelings and thoughts at that moment. For now, I have to concentrate all my energy on my duties. I say Bye to that soldier and head the direct way to my accommodation. Arriving there I can´t hold it back any longer. For the first time in my life as a soldier I am overwhelmed by feelings of fear and helplessness. I can´t hold back the tears.

I am alone in the tent. After some time I dry my tears and take care of my documents.

An hour later I meet my boss from the J4 section, Major K. in the MWR tent. We´re discussing some topics regarding the hand over with our predecessors. During the conversation I don´t mention any word of Christian's death. I cannot because I can´t even believe it. It just can´t be true. He is the second person I lost while being absent. First my grandma whom I was very close to. I wasn't able to be there either when it happened. And now Christian too was dragged out of my life without giving me the chance to say good bye. How many more will I lose?

Grief in the first hours

5. Every day camp life

I n the following weeks we take over the duties from our predecessors. As mentioned before, my main duty in this first mission is a logistics administrator. A job that is mainly done in front of a desk and requires an awful lot of phone calls. But at least during my inspections of the individual subunits I was able to recognize and solve issues and take care of a lack of material in direct contact with the ones in need.

Regarding our predecessors' organisation of procedures, the ones that proved to be effective we kept. Other things were adjusted or let´s say improved to our requirements. Best example we had to face for the need of improvement was the topic fuel. Once having a closer look to the books, we found out that there was quite a difference between the amounts given out stated in the reports and the real amounts missing.

That time I got to get in touch with a LTC of the Civil Military Cooperation (CIMIC), Armin F. He was brought to Kabul just for a few weeks to replace an CIMIC Officer being on leave. It was his second deployment to Afghanistan. We got along quite well from the very first day. Like being on the same page. We even found out that both of us were stationed in the same BN back home but at different times. I got the same positive feeling with Armin like I had with Christian before.

Since Armin was doing his job mainly outside and I basically inside the camp we only had chance to catch up in the evening for a drink in the MWR tent and talk about the day. Armin had an interesting job at CIMIC and understood quickly what his major tasks were and in fact also why we were in this country and what our main goals were: To advise and help its people rebuild their land in every meaning of the word.

Armin told me about our Forward Operating Bases (FOB) and outposts which were also run with the fuel I was responsible for. We agreed on a trip to these outposts to give me the opportunity to get my own picture of the situation. Shortly after I reported this idea to my commander and received the order for a drive to KUNDUZ area. It will be my first mission outside the safe walls of the camp.

As soon as you want to leave the camp with a vehicle you need a driving order with a detailed description of the route. The reason for that is simple. The command staff need to be informed at all times which forces are moving or where they are located in order to be able to coordinate them or others if needed. Therefore, it is also mandatory to report your status every hour.

Due to Armin´s vehicle already being packed with him, two other soldiers and the interpreter (a local Afghan person who is able to translate the Afghan languages and whose background is checked by our military counter intelligence service), I had to join the convoy with my own vehicle. Before starting we had a detailed brief about the route, how to act in various threatening situations and our individual roles in case of enemy contact.

The first planned destination would be the ALI-ABAD outpost where the German Bundeswehr was operating together with Afghan national police. That is the first place where they use the mentioned fuel operated generators I wanted to take a look at. After that we planned to go to a printing house in POL-E-KHOMRI that was printing flyers for the upcoming elections of the afghan parliament. From there we would head back to our camp.

Next morning at 0900 we get ready to deploy. I put on my bullet proof vest, my helmet, lock and load my rifle, do a radio check and move to the vehicles waiting already with running engines. We start. The afghan guards are opening the gates and we turn on the main exit road. The holes on the way are as big as truck tires and I have to drive carefully to avoid them. The streets are full. Not filled with cars but with donkey carts. Children playing in the street holes filled with yesterdays' rain. "Wow, what a cool pool!" comes to my mind in the first place. But shortly after I realize how sad this picture actually is. How sad it is that these children don't have proper playgrounds.

The tour is done without any negative inncidents and we arrive back at camp late evening. The following days will be packed with lots of work. Due to the mentioned elections our contingent gets stocked up both in personnel and material. To house the planned amount of people we had to rearrange certain structures of the camp. I knew that in nearby future such short notice requirements won't be a problem anymore since the new depot at the airport was almost done and was about to become operational at the beginning of 2006.
Since the beginning of the ISAF mission in 2001 not only did the manpower increased over and over again, but also the combat equipment and all the support related material, which of course, had to be stocked up multiple times.

Regarding all my tasks already described, you can imagine how fast the time went by. Days, weeks and months were just flying by. Sometimes strange things happened along the not so thrilling everyday tasks, like containers which were actually addressed to KABUL suddenly turning up at our camp while others addressed to us somehow popped up in FEYZABAD.
But sometimes and all of a sudden good things also happen. One day I could not believe my eyes when

Bridadier General A. shows up for inspecting the unit and I recognize him to be that Officer from back then tasting cake fudge in my field kitchen years ago. Now and then I also got the chance to join the transportation platoon at the airport and help them to load and unload the arriving and departing airlifters. There are airlifters coming in every day and night. This work takes a whole day although the airport is only less than 8 km away. Since the inspection of the transportation platoon is also part of my main duties I started to use this opportunity to get out of the camp as often as possible for a little variation.

A few days later I got the chance to join the supply transportation flight to FEYZABAAD with a Sikorsky CH-53 helicopter that I was more than happy about in order to get some new impressions. FEYZABAD is about 1200 meters above zero.

waiting for material from Germany

Normally, supply transportation is made via local so-called jingle trucks on the land route. For the distance of 240 km these trucks need about eight to ten hours because of the poor road conditions, you just cannot compare them to the ones back home. But on these routes, it is not possible to transport sensitive or dangerous material. In these cases, airlift capacities are used. The flight proceeds without any incidents. I am placed next to the door gunner to secure the zone to the back and below the helicopter.

The CH-53 is flying as low as possible over fields and mountain tops and offers us an incredible view on the afghan nature. Once landed we stay only half an hour till everything is unloaded and loaded with stuff for us and head back immediately to KUNDUZ. It´s already noon when we arrive at the airport and it´s awfully hot, feeling like 45 degrees Celsius or more. Once our material and field mail is unloaded I receive a cold bottle of water which I gratefully empty within seconds. At home I have to force down every sip, but in Afghanistan I drank 4 to 5 liters for sure.

flight with CH-53 to Feyzabad

6. Support from Austria

I n addition to all our tasks there was another huge challenge that had an effect on all of us. The Afghan elections on the 18th of September. They were the first free elections for this country's people since 1988 in which they had to vote for the 249 seats in the parliament as well as for the provincial authorities. For the first time women were also given the right to vote and to run for the representing positions. Among the 2800 candidates were 330 women. Due to the threats by the Taliban, other terrorist militias and opposing forces against these elections the ISAF forces had the order to secure the preparation and execution of these elections. Therefore, we received support by the Austrian Response Forces Team (AUCON3 / ISAF). This Austrian contingent consisted of 85 men and was put under German command. For the duration of their mission they were hosted by us in the camp.

The teamwork with our Austrian comrades was characterized by professionalism and yes, you may call it harmony, which was clearly due to a similar cultural background and both our nations speaking the same language. My impression was confirmed by Armin who had to work with them outside the camp on a daily basis and like me had the chance to join my Austrian colleagues for patrolling KUNDUZ city one time.
This patrol was one of the most intense experiences I had outside the base. We began our way from the

direction of the Atzbeigi Mosque, along the Spinzar company which was the biggest supplier for cotton in whole Afghanistan those days. The people, especially the youngsters and the children greeted us in heartwarming ways, giving us the feeling of being welcome. It's a wonderful but also strange feeling that is spreading through my whole body thinking of what we were told during pre-mission training of being in the back sight every moment of our mission. I have to mention that in those days it was possible for us to perform patrols without heavily armored vehicles. This changed rapidly the following years.

Austrian soldiers on patrol

One of the most fascinating things was the alignment of the streets where the merchants were offering their goods. It was so different from how it is at home, where you have stores or the weekly markets, where there is one tent with fruits and vegetables and at another you would find cheese. In Afghanistan you have one street where you find fabric of all variations and colours. Another only for all types of meat. Another only with coal and wood. And so on and so on. Heads of cow and sheep hanging in front of doors or being presented on tables. As said, it is absolutely incomparable with Europe.

Being as different as it is, it's working out well. Goods are cooled with ice cubes as it was done for hundreds of years. Being a qualified cook, my heart bet like hell when I saw and smelled all those exotic seasonings offered in one of the streets. The Pakistani / Indian influence is obvious in the afghan culinary culture. The most favored seasoning in afghan cuisine is Garam Masala, which is a mixture of Safron, Cinnamon, Mint, Caraway seed, Pepper and Chili. Other much appreciated seasonings in Afghanistan such as Dill, Coriander and Cloves are proof of the Persian and Arabic influence. This country could be a paradise to me, if it was not for the serious cause of my presence there.

A few days later I got the opportunity to go to the city's market for "shopping" along with my interpreter. I had to buy wood for some construction work that had to be done in the
camp.

spice market in Kunduz, a paradise for cooks

The translator wears the national costume. I am clearly recognizable as a soldier in my uniform. I'm obviously the stranger. I'm getting scared for a moment. I realize that something could happen to me. The unknown dark faces with their long beards are watching every step we make. The security situation then was very uncertain. A stay on this market was definitely not safe. As it turns out later, my feeling was not unfounded, but this day the uneasy feeling in my stomach remained without consequences. In hindsight, I probably worried too much. This day would be the last one I felt this kind of fear.

The impressions of this day remain in my memory in every detail. In the coming days, weeks and months I will experience situations that are similarly threatening, but which I will not experience as intensively as on this particular day. But such thoughts and feelings about possible threats should be quickly forgotten when you are on a mission. One just has to walk through the streets with open eyes and a sharp mind.

The amazing thing about Afghanistan is that its people are very hospitable and friendly to strangers. They condemn the attacks of the terrorists the same way as the rest of the world does.

It is a shame that due to the war these people cannot do more for their country like developing tourism. In my eyes, this wonderful country and its people deserve it.

Street vendor of flatbread in Kunduz

7. A baker and his flatbread

There is an Afghan baker near the camp where you can buy fresh bread every day, except on Fridays. While the flatbreads are in the oven, they are moistened several times with green tea. This is quite straight forward; the baker just takes some sips of tea in his mouth and sprays the tea on the bread. This generates the necessary humidity for the bread. At the end, the bread is sprinkled with salt, which gives them a spicy touch.

Despite of this unusual production method, it had become a tradition for us soldiers to eat there together every Saturday evening, and on this occasion this bread is eaten with pleasure. Additionally, we also put some specialties from home on the table.

It is actually very idyllic sometimes, which one probably cannot imagine. We sit at our table in front of our hut protected by trees and shrubs. In front of us on the table are the fresh flatbread, sliced bacon and ham from the black forest as well as homemade canned liver sausage, smoked blood sausage and fresh paprika, cucumbers and garlic.

We do this every Saturday evening with the COY commander, the first sergeant and other comrades. For a short time, it feels like holiday and we forget that we are on a mission in a war-torn land.

8. At the medic`s

On my daily round through the camp I visit various departments to see if everything is OK. Today I focus especially on the supply group that will receive a new load of barbed wire for the outer camp wall. Besides that, I am waiting for a lot of spare parts for our vehicles.

From a distance, I already see the truck of an Afghan transport company. I watch briefly as the truck is unloaded and checked by the supervising NCO of the supply group if all parts we have ordered were on board or whether I will have to make a phone call like so many times before.

Suddenly I hear the siren of the ambulance and two other vehicles of the security company leaving the camp. I keep on concentrating on the unloading of the truck. Half an hour later I make my way to my office and hear from other comrades that there was an attack in Kunduz. That moment it was not clear if there were Germans among the victims.

I sit in my office feeling bad. The recce squad that had left the camp this morning still isn't back. When my boss enters my office, I turn to him asking immediately if he has any news. He does not. Further information has not been spread so far. The security component though requested additional personnel.

Sometime later we hear the sirens of a bunch of ambulances entering the camp. There are definitely a lot of casualties I think to myself. We often witness the procedures of wounded being brought to the camp, so we know that our medics take their job seriously and handle it professionally.

At about 1900 I have to meet with the air logistics supervisor to coordinate the loadings for the upcoming day. On the way to him I pass the surgery containers of our medics and watch some red fluid leaving the containers drain hole forming a puddle at the back side of it. That means that our medics had some awful work to do. The thought of me lying on their table one day makes me shiver.

Passing the containers I see two military doctors smoking cigarettes. They were shaking their heads mentioning an afghan police officer being wounded very badly in the attack. I know it should not matter, but in that moment, I am so glad to hear that it was not one of our guys. I am also glad to hear that the afghan police officer has survived.

A few days later I am invited for coffee at the medics'. When I enter the front tent, I see an afghan boy coming up to me. He holds an inflated rubber glove with a smiling face drawn on it with a pen in his hand. The boy is laughing and seems to have so much fun with his "toy". I see a sign saying "coffee corner" and approach it, when the boy somehow stands directly in front of me. He stretches out his hand in my direction holding his rubber glove balloon. I wink at him passing by saying what a lovely balloon he has. The glance in his eyes fascinating me that much that I turn around to him again. What I see shakes me to the bones. Only now I recognize that he is just wearing a surgery shirt exposing his back. Where every healthy person would have buttocks there was just a hole. The pelvic bones were completely revealed under his skin and all the muscles were gone. Whilst playing with a "butterfly mine", his buttocks were blown off.

There are still thousands of these mines lying around everywhere. To the children they just look like unsuspicious toys. The boy I saw is one of so many examples of how dangerous these toys are. This picture will be planted in my head for all times.

A friend of mine from the medics told me that this boy already had ten surgeries and will have to face a few more. Despite his heavy injuries the boy is so incredibly happy and has a love for life that he shows the medical personnel every single day. I just hope that one day he will have a life worth living. Therefore, I wish him all the best.

entrance tot he emergency

A jungle truck brings material out of Kabul

9. Earthquake in Pakistan

Saturday October 8th, 7 AM. Saturdays actually always offer the possibility to stay in bed a bit longer …but not today. Due to the J4 section being accommodated in a clay building our private as well as our duty rooms are located in the same facility. For the Saturday duties we do weekly shifts because its weekend in Germany. That's why on Saturdays and Sundays there is nothing we can do if it is related to support for the PRT from Germany.

But today I am startled out of my coziness quite harshly. My field bed is shaking and the dry clay is crumbling from the roof directly on my face. I jump off my bed immediately and run out. At least I try to. The ground is shaking as heavily as if you would run on raw eggs. In that very moment I realize: it's an earthquake.

It's the first earthquake I experience live myself. It only takes a few minutes and suddenly it's all calm again. Only a few light aftermaths are to follow. Nothing really serious. But just a few minutes later we receive the message that the north of Pakistan hasn't been that lucky. The region was hit by a quake of 7,6 on the scale with an epicenter only 50 kilometers away from its capital ISLAMABAD leaving large areas fully destroyed.

The regions of Afghanistan, Pakistan and India have been struck by earthquakes quite often in the past. But this time it was unusually heavy and brought seemingly endless destruction and suffering to the people concerned.

Heavy earthquake in northern Pakistan in 2005

Within moments our assignment turns into a humanitarian support mission for the victims of this catastrophe. It takes only a few hours for the German Bundeswehr to provide a support package of Soldiers and Materials to be sent to Pakistan. On the very same day 2 additional CH-53 transport helicopters are sent on rescue and support missions to MUZAFFARABAD. In the following days they will provide tons of food, tents, a water treatment plant, thousands of blankets, 1.5 tons of medication, thousands of MREs and much more to the people in desperate need. Unfortunately, the efforts of all the other nations will save 80.000 people from dying from this horrific catastrophe.

The map on our office wall shows how close to Afghanistan the earthquake actually happened. According to internal reports our guys in FEYZABAD felt the quake obviously much more intense than us in KUNDUZ. What I had witnessed here myself was more than enough to imagine the horror that the Pakistanis had to face on this day. At least we are here in the right place and at the right time to save many people from starving and also becoming homeless in such a tuff environment.

It's odd. At home you watch the news and see these kinds of pictures and hidden inside you think to yourself: thank God these things never happen over here. But being here, only less than one hundred kilometers away from its epicenter...feeling it right in your bones and stomach. It makes you feel related to all these suffering people and you can't stop thinking and imagining how much worse it was for them being closer to the disaster and its aftermaths.

At lunch time I meet with Armin. The only topic we speak about is the earthquake. But he too has only heard the same information as I already got. And like me he is asking himself why it always has to be the ones who already have nothing who suffer the most. We both know there will never be an answer to that.Despite the earthquake in the morning the rest of the day is developing normally. All of us do our business as usual. At the end of the day I meet with Armin again and we are playing some "Kicker" to get rid of those negative thoughts. Armin tells me about his day which was dominated by a project outside the camp that he had to support. He describes his actual tasks and role. As a CIMIC officer he is getting in contact with majors and elders of regions and villages in our AOR in order to inform them about projects from our PRT forces. This could be for example the establishing of a new or additional police station or other security facilities. It is mostly not necessary to beg for their support because most of them are happy for every infrastructural support they can get. And of course there is the fact that basically every project is in need of local companies' and workers' support and this is the main step to prosperity.

Of course, these CIMIC soldiers aren't going out on such missions on their own. They are always accompanied by protection teams of our army. Such a convoy consist of at least about 30 German soldiers on 2 DINGO armored combat vehicles, 3 FUCHS armored personnel carriers of which one is specially equipped with devices to disturb radio signal activated IEDs and one to function as an armored medics rescue vehicle. Furthermore, this convoy will be accompanied by 2 pickups of the Afghan National Police (ANP) with 12 riflemen.

Before that I had no clue what the CIMIC guys actually do. Armin asks me if I would like to accompany them next time to have a look myself at how they operate.

Already a few days later we are able to make it possible for me to come with them. I join the CIMIC team to check the status of project "School". It's always interesting to see how the population is accepting our help and that of other organizations. Project "School" is about a girls' school that was attacked and destroyed by the Taliban. By destroying that school, the enemy also burned down the chances for education and therefore a better life for the girls in that region. To give these kids back the opportunity to learn, the school is rebuilt by local companies with our support. The progress is already quite visible and you can see the main walls. One of the things that impresses me the most is how these workers are able to carry out all the tasks with the simplest tools and the total absence of modern devices. Calculating is done in the sand. As a spirit level they used a hose filled with a certain amount of water. Absolutely amazing.

The following days pass by quickly and Armin has to go to KABUL before he leaves for Germany 14 days later. At that time for me there were less than 8 days till my assignment ends. We agree that we definitely have to catch up back in good old Germany. On our last evening together we relax in the garden in front of our MWR tent and chat about the one or other weird comrade or the stupid behavior of some officers and how we see the world. Nonsense basically. In that moment none of us has even the tiniest idea what is about to come up in the near future. Like always when it comes to say farewell to a comrade I personally know I am already waiting for Armin in the early morning at the market. He is in a good mood of course. Happy that it's only a few days left separating him from home and his loved ones. He gets in the MUNGO turns back to me and says: "Keep your head down!" I wave my hand for good bye. After he landed in KABUL he calls me from his duty phone to report that he is fine. The day before I have to leave Afghanistan he calls me and we are looking forward to meet back home. It will be or very last conversation. Forever.

The 14th of November is the day when I am about to leave KUNDUZ. It's a lovely day. The sun shines brightly and warm. At 0900 hours we fly with the CH-53 from KUNDUZ to TERMEZ in Uzbekistan. At 1400 hours I take the MoD Airbus to STUTTGART. I am so looking forward to be home! I can't wait to get there. Suddenly these feelings of joy and happiness get mixed with a strange uncomfortable feeling. That feeling shall become a presentiment which is to be followed by an ugly certainty. While I am flying to STUTTGART Armin's Vehicle within the convoy is rammed by a vehicle borne IED. The blast is so immense that Armin dies immediately while 2 other soldiers of the same vehicle are heavily injured but at least alive. It's the second comrade of mine I personally know to sacrifice his life on a mission for his fatherland.

I still have these pictures of Christian and Armin in my mind. I will keep them there for the rest of my life.

mourning party for Armin who fell in Kabul

10. My time in between the missions

We landed safely in STUTTGART where my nowadays ex-wife and Marco were already waiting for me. On the way home, 40km before we arrived, my head started spinning and thoughts came up about everything I had witnessed, so that I was not even able to feel happy about being home. Of course, I tried to hide the fact. I needed some time to get acclimatised to this rapid change of environment. Nevertheless, I immediately started to work again. There have been a lot of changes to personnel circumstances during my absence which I had to adapt to. Everything seemed somehow different and when I got a new job offer I decided to change my employer and start something new. I became the Team Bus Driver for the Gerolstein-Sports-Bicycle Team. I got a bus driver license and from 2006 on, I drove the Athletes from town to town throughout Europe. From competitions classics like the Paris-Nizza to regular one day tournaments like Paris Roubaix (250km) to the highlights like Giro d'Italia, Tour de France or the Vuelta a Espana. In those days, bicycle sports were also very famous in Germany. It was the time before all those doping affairs ruined these unique competitions. I have to admit that I was addicted to bicycle racing sports. However, I never got beyond the amateurs' class. But this fact definitely had its part in me being so satisfied with my new assignment.

In the following two years I saw a lot of the world, especially of Europe. Both years we were on the road from February to October and I was away from home quite a lot, but it was an experience that I would not want to miss. Unfortunately, this adventure ended soon after the season of 2008.

waiting at the finish in the french Pau

11. Second deployment

My next mission deployment came 5 years later in the year 2010. A lot happened during that time. I had various reserve assignments in Germany, but slid into a phase of my life no one desires for. I was unemployed.

To avoid hanging around and doing nothing, I again volunteered for a mission deployment and was lucky. I got the position of military driver and assistant to the cultural adviser of the mission contingent command. What I had to expect from this assignment was not clear to me the moment I agreed. Before I could leave for the mission, I was sent to the Centre for Operative Communication in MEYEN, which you may call something like a Psy-Ops Command and Training Centre of the German armed forces. There I was introduced to Lieutenant Colonel M., who outlined to me my future duties and tasks. Lieutenant Colonel M. was also my commanding officer then and once we reached the mission area. He was to become the cultural adviser (IEB) both for the Commander Regional Command North as well as for the German mission contingent ISAF. The main tasks of the IEB officer are to discuss information, contacts and decisions concerning the cultural aspects of a mission, operations with ISAF forces and the local population and to support finding proper solutions. My tasks as the

IEB sergeant would be all the administrative aspects of support for our duties, to manage our whole working environment and to escort and secure my commanding officer as his driver. After all preparations, tests and training had been successfully concluded, there were only a few days left until the deployment.

This time again with the helicopter

12. The next flight to Afganistan

This time, I am not joining a whole company, but going on a mission accompanied only by the Officer from MAYEN who later would become the cultural adviser in FEYZABAD. I am brought to the Air Base COLOGNE / WAHN by my ex-wife a day prior to the departure flight and we stay at a hotel in the vicinity of the base to avoid any stress right before the flight. In the time before the check-in starts we enjoy some coffee and a small breakfast at the waiting lounge.

At 11:45 hours the check-in starts and I drop my so-called mission crate and sea bag on the counter. After all administrative formalities are done I accompany my wife to her car to say farewell. When I watch her leave, some divided feelings come up and I turn away, heading back to the terminal. I am so looking forward for what is waiting for me, but at the same moment I know I won't see my family again for 6 long months. But same as with my first deployment I still have this feeling of doing the right thing for the right cause.

The boarding begins at 12:00 hours and we enter the bus that brings us to our plane, which waits on the runway. This time it's all routine. Again, it is an Airbus A310 that again will first drop us at TERMEZ before we will do our final approach to MAZAR-I-SHARIF in Afghanistan. Right on time at 12:30 hours the A310 lifts off and I am about to "meet" with Uzbekistan soon.

We land late that evening and the unavoidable procedures of in-processing starts. Like last time they collect all our military IDs and the travel passports of the civilian personnel. Since I am already familiar with this I drop a joke to the guy on the seat next to me saying that the kind Uzbek officer actually just needs to have a look at his files from 2005 where he should have a copy of my passport already. Still grinning, I realize the officer is staring at me with a rather unpleasant impression. I immediately become serious and look down, hoping that guy would not be one of those understanding German. Funny enough, this time the procedure is performed much faster than back then and I wonder if it might have been my joke forcing them to shorten this whole process.

Shortly after we are allowed to leave the aircraft to be picked up by a bus bringing us to our assembly point where we will get briefed about the next flight bringing us to MAZAR-I-SHARIF the next morning.

After the obligatory greetings by assigned personnel of the Air Base, we are shown to our luggage which we are to place on pallets labeled with our various destinations. After that we are brought to our accommodation containers where we may rest for the night. Compared to the tents I had to use last time and which I could still see all around the base, these containers are pure luxury. This time, we are the lucky ones. After arranging my bed for the night, I go over to the MWR tent. I switch my mobile from flight mode to regular and send my first SMS home since I arrived here. Just a short one letting my loved ones know that I am fine.

the gate to Termez

In the morning we have a good breakfast and leave TERMEZ by an C160 heading for MAZAR-I-SHARIF, which is the fourth largest city in Afghanistan right after KABUL, HERAT, KANDAHAR. It is also the capital of the district bearing the same name as well as the capital of the province of BALKH. Arriving in MAZA (مزار شریف), as we all call it, I am picked up by Sergeant 1st class Sven F. who is responsible for providing everything the PsyOps working environment needs. I realize his talent for this important task immediately as he knows exactly who's who of the camp's supply chain.

He shows me my accommodation where I am going to stay until the container room is free for the rest of my time here. He then lets me get familiar with my working environment which is located at the ring road right next to the building of the military police. Sometime later during the mission we will be relocated to an extra separated and fenced area of the camp which will carry the name "PsyOps".

We take a ride through the camp and Sven shows me around. The medical facility and the hospital, the Norwegian compound, the so called international "Marketender" which is something like a supermarket where you can get tax free stuff only approved to soldiers. Everything a soldier desires can be found there. From combat gloves to toothpaste; they have it all. No matter the nationality, every ISAF soldier is allowed to purchase what he needs. After the Norwegian compound we go to the garage which has separate departments for the inspection and repairing of both military vehicle as well as the civilian ones which are leased from I-don't-know-who. After that we pay a visit to the Post office and the German national "Marketender" which is located close to the German kitchen.

The ride takes quite some time. The camp is just huge. With its 300 hectares it is the largest camp of the international alliance in Afghanistan and this size doesn't even include the space assigned to US forces, which is established in 2010.

After the ride it is time to get some lunch. Sven shows me where to get it, only this time we go there by foot. On the way he shows me where to drop my laundry. The canteen hall is wide. At the peak up to 4500 soldiers and civil advisers have to be served here. This day there are just a few around so that I can have a closer look to who is joining us.

After lunch I go to the main gate where an admin office is located in order to get my accreditation done. This is done surprisingly fast. You just provide your official mission orders and a picture is made. With these documents they create an ID with information like the duration of your stay and the date of your out-processing. That ID is to be worn visible all the time you are on the move within the camp.

view from the dining room to the living container

After these formalities I go back to my provisory accommodation to sort it a little. Not too cozy, since I am going to leave it for my assigned container room in a short while, but just as nice as possible to be able to relax. Late afternoon I leave my temporary "apartment" to meet Sven who provides me with my in-processing execution checklist which will force me to run to all the stations in order to get stuff and signatures as I have already experienced during my last mission. In addition to all the annoying administrative things, the in-processing includes a briefing for the rules concerning behavior when leaving / operating outside the camp environment and the dress code at various occasions.

Furthermore, there is an additional counter IED training where the most updated information and procedures of that topic are taught to the soldiers. They even have an exercise environment within the camp where you can train to detect the various types of IEDs to be found in our area of operation. We, of course, had some counter IED briefings back home too, but besides the fact that in Germany they just didn't have the assets to teach us practically, I am a fan of getting the things taught on base. The closest training you can get is the one in your actual mission environment.

Done with the bunch of tasks I had for this day, I go to meet Sven for dinner. When I pick him up at his office we walk to the canteen and he informs me that my boss, Lieutenant Colonel M., has arrived. The rest of the team shall come much later in August. Until then, I will be quite busy with planning the mentioned relocation of our service to its newly assigned area and of course the handover takeover has to be organized, too.

13. Preparation for handover

Normaly a handover is done by your predecessor, the guy who was doing your job before you came. Over here it was different.

When LTC M. was in TERMEZ waiting for his flight to MAZAR, 1st Lieutenant NAVY H. and my boss met for a chat.

The 1st Lieutenant had a few days of leave und wanted to take care of a few things back in Germany.

The two officers barely have the time to discuss the timings for the arrivals and the handover takeover schedule.

In a few days the move will take place and it's me who has to prepare and execute the arrival of the one as well as the departure of the other. I don't waste any time and start by collecting boxes for all the things of the predecessor like maps, office items and folders. His private stuff I pack in separate boxes with his name on.

The days until the 1st Lieutenants returns from his short trip pass by very fast and -1 2 3-, it's time to pick him up from the airport. I brought him to his accommodation first to give him the chance to rest a little. Arriving there, he is saying that we will see each other in less than a hour to discuss further issues concerning the handover. Lieutenant Colonel M. joins us one and half hours later. Somehow the whole discussion appears to become quite difficult due to the fact that previously made agreements by the two officers were not met as wished by both of them. I feel that the tensions are raising and before it escalates I try to calm both of them down, which somehow worked.

Unfortunately, in the aftermath of the mentioned discussion the 1st Lieutenant does not recognize the LTC as a fellow soldier anymore and even less as a team member. The situation is actually ridiculous considering the fact that we are in a war zone and that we all should fight on the same side. This gives my boss, the LTC, quite a tough time and me even more since I am sitting right between the two and have to serve both of them at the same level. As an experienced Sergeant rank I know exactly how to deal with a handover takeover but how to handle this weird "Mickey Mouse-I-don't -wanna-play-with-him-bull shit" was never part of my training at all.

Nevertheless, I try my best to bring this handover take over to a successful end which by a miracle I somehow achieve without any serious issues despite the horrible administrative paper war. Actually, I had a good connection to the 1st Lieutenant and close to his leave we even agreed on address each other by a "Du" which is a form in the German language that you only use amongst friends. The day of the 1st Lieutenants farewell from Afghanistan has come and of course it's me picking him up and accompanying him to the airport. We have a coffee together in the waiting hall. We´re bullshitting a little until it's time for the boarding.

When the speakers announce his flight we say good bye and he jumps on the jeep bringing him to the C-160.

With this C160 he flew away

14. Challenges at the IEB-Cell

After the 1st Lieutenant has left I start with my duty for the day. The change of command of the ISAF- commander is about to happen. Everyone knows already who the new one is going to be. This new commander is widely known for his detailed and precise instructions about everyone's individual tasks and the goals he is aiming to achieve.

Our new working environment, the so called "Regional PsyOps Support Element", consists of various sections and sub elements like the "mission camera teams" about which I am going to share some details later. Furthermore, there are the sections of Video-production which is producing "Information Movies", and the TAA, whose task it is to collect information about the feelings and views of the local population regarding our forces mission. These guys are in contact with the local population on a daily basis and having the chance to even get in touch with things like women housings where women can move around freely without male company.

The TAA guys are responsible for an updated picture of the emotional aspects of our mission concerning the local population, to assure a cultural exchange and to establish trust between us the mission personnel and the local population. In order to achieve these goals, they constantly meet with the people in their homes as well as in public

spaces like the so called "women's garden" in KA-
BUL.

Besides these meetings with individuals there are
of course fix counterparts or let's say mandatory
partners for exchange and discussions like representatives from the BALKH University, Students
of the Teachers Training Centers TT, local mayors,
elders and directors of local children's asylums.
When it comes to these kinds of meetings, the
RPOSE of course supports the TAA teams with
material as well as with personnel. For example,
when I once volunteered as a driver and additional security personnel for them.

The next morning I meet my new boss for the first
time here in Afghanistan. We sit down for a coffee
in our container and discuss the tasks for the
week.

Since my boss is going to be occupied with instructions and planning meetings, it will be my
workload to take care of the moving and other or-
ganizational tasks. Apart from the fact that I am
not yet done with my own in processing; I feel
that after our chat at least I know what the boss
has in mind and can start with the preparations.
The first thing I do is to order us a TOYOTA
4Runner SUV via the J4 branch. The German
Army rents these types of cars from an Afghan
contractor company. We, of course, need an armored one. Therefore, they bring it to DUBAI in
the UAE. After that armor upgrade the whole vehicle is like 5 tons heavy. Sure you cannot compare it with quality work back in Germany but it

meets the standards and back then there was no other option for us. That car will bring us to the heads appointments over here as well as in KUNDUZ or FEYZABAD, for which we are both responsible for as well.

The rest of the day I find out where the sections are located and with whom I will have to cooperate with in the next months. I will get to know a lot of different people: From backers to police chiefs up to the governor of the province BALKH. Together with my fellow soldiers from the PsyOps team I accomplish the moving of our cell from the old to the new location. The whole thing takes us three days. The following days we collect and create new maps, informational sheets and standardized forms for the IEB cell.

Two days later we are "combat ready" and finally can start to our work. The other sections have moved too. I like to pass by the media guys to sneak in and have a look how they create these info films which I was always fascinated by.

Sven's office is only two doors away so that I can get in touch with him in no time. When the day is over, Sven and I finish the duty with a dinner. On the way to the canteen we always chat about the day and come to the conclusion, that we actually did a good job. To bring this moving of such a huge branch to a successful end in that short space of time is definitely something to be proud of. The days are just running by and I am sure I will be able to handle everything until the support in form of additional personnel will arrive which is expected to happen in two months time.

At home, such pictures are no longer visible

15. Visit tot he police chief at the airport

Our first mission outside the safe walls of the camp is to meet up with the local police chief Mr. Latif at the civil part of the airport of MAZAR-I-SHARIF in order to establish the first contact. First thing I noticed when we arrived was that they kept us waiting for quite some time until they finally let us through to the chief, although we had been right on time for the scheduled appointment. Later I learned that this "keeping you waiting" is kind of a cultural rule in this country and somehow a sign of respect. It seems the more important a person is, the longer you have to wait.

As said after quite some time of waiting for his "excellency", his, let's say "secretary", came out and kindly asks us to follow him. We enter the chief's office where the he is sitting in an enormous throne-like armchair in front of a ridiculously huge wooden table. The man gets up and greets us with the typical afghan gesture of putting his right hand to his heart with the words "Salam Aleikum" -may peace be with you-. We reply with the same greeting and sit down on the offered chairs. Our "terp" (interpreter) translates the phrases of greetings of my boss. During the conversation of the two officers I have the chance to look around the office and get an impression of what a bad shape the whole airport structure must be in. The paint on the walls has faded, the carpets on the floor are dirty and ripped off in various spots and that smell crawling in to my nose for sure did not come from rotten flowers. I remind myself of KUNDUZ and remembered that tidiness is obviously not the first priority in this country. 15 minutes later a servant enters the office holding a tablet with four glasses which don't really look like they came directly out of the dishwasher. He slowly fills them with tea and passes them on to each of us. I thank him and take small sips from the glass, avoiding to think of the various bacteria I am swallowing with each drop. But I have to admit, the tea was just excellent. An afghan green tea of highest quality. Instead of cookies as a complimentary like we Europeans use to serve on such an occasion, they serve you nuts here. The conversation lasted round about 45 minutes. After saying farewell, we depart directly back to camp MARMAL. On the way back, I think about the airport police chiefs appearance, which reminded me more of a drug lord than an high ranking police officer. Not really a trustworthy aura, I thought to myself. I would never mention my thoughts about him to anyone. With these kinds of people over here you better be on good terms, if you want to get through in one piece.

Back in our office we recapitulate the meeting with Mr. Latif and try to filter out the most important information which my Lieutenant Colonel wants to brief the General about later. I create a list of the various appointments, POCs and the main outcome in order to provide a clear picture of who spoke when about what in case it's needed.

In the evening a service is held for the German soldiers of Airborne Bataillon 373 who died in an ambush by the Taliban on 15th of April 2010, which until then was one of the fiercest engagements the German Army was ever involved in since Worldwar II. The attack was planned, coordinated and executed in such a professional manner, never before experienced by the NATO forces of RC North, it led to awful losses for the involved unit. Four soldiers lost their lives during the battle and many more were heavily wounded and crippled for the rest of their lives.

A lot of technical equipment and vehicles were destroyed and lost to the enemy.

The numbers of terrorist operations and so-called suicide attacks had rose significantly since 2005, which of cause affected the security situation in the whole area of operation dramatically. This increase of the enemies' activities was made obvious to me only a couple of days after the service for the fallen paratroopers, when I again had to attend a funeral service for four fellow Norwegian soldiers, who were killed by an IED while being on the way to a recce mission in the area of MEYMANEH. It is an horrible feeling every time you see the coffins passing by while you stand along the designated road for the ceremony and give the fallen the last salute. I still remember the four pickup trucks carrying each of the four coffins covered in their national flag.

In front of the trucks a soldier carries a photograph

of the fallen. Another soldier is following him carrying a pillow with all the medals the soldier had achieved so far along with those combat mission- and NATO medals they earned in the mission they died in. You look to the framed pictures with the black band in the upper right corner and can't stand asking yourself what happy life they would have had ahead of them, if they hadn't come here to sacrifice it. But the worst thing is to look into the eyes of the soldiers accompanying the dead and read in their faces that there is only pain and misery left. I get touched by that every single time, even though the killed were not familiar to me. In my eyes, every soldier serving a mission is my brother.

Sadly, I had to see this picture way to often

16. First tasks fort he new unit

Since June 16th, all the handover trials are finished, so everybody's mind is free of stress and therefore receptible for new tasks. The last days and weeks had been quite challenging and work-intensive, like the listing of all the warlords in the provinces of Balch, Faizabad, Baghlan, Herat and all the other 30 provinces of Afghanistan.

The first intercultural task was visiting the HERON flight unit, where former fighter pilots work, but instead of jets they now operate drones from the ground. Tobias gives them a lecture about what intercultural life means in this country, so they can assess certain situations better via air reconnaissance.

After the lecture, the pilots are allowed to ask questions, for example when prayer times are for the Muslims and who is most likely to fetch water for the family. What do Afghan people do after the last prayer of the day? Do the farmers work in the fields even at night? What is typical behavior for the local population and what is not? How can attacks be prevented? Are accumulations of motorcycles in rural areas suspicious? Those were the questions of the pilots, so they can do a proper interpretation of the aerial photographs and the live pictures.

During the first weeks, our main tasks were making Ramadan cards and flyers with important information, which included descriptions in several languages of the right behavior during Ramadan when being outside the gates. It was supposed to be a pocket card, so that every soldier could look up the rules how to act during this time. More than 10.000 of those cards were printed and distributed to RC NORTH, PRT KUNDUZ, PRT FEYZABAD as well as to our allies from Norway, Sweden, Hungary, Serbia and Montenegro, so every soldier had the same guidelines how the act during this time.

The next task for Tobias is visiting the intercultural mission advisor in Kunduz. We arrive via C-160 Transall transfer from Mazar-e-Sharif - Kunduz to the first information event. Our comrades from IEB pick us up from the Kunduz airport and drive us to the camp.

First, they give us a tour around the camp, after that they show us our tent for the night. From the tent, we go to the office where the information event with the subsequent brainstorming is taking place. It is quite interesting to learn what happens in and around Kunduz and what the people think about us. After 30 years of war, not everything can be rebuilt and put in order in such a short space of time, despite the many efforts currently taking place to do exactly that. As we all know, Rome also wasn't built in a day. But we make a little progress every day and that is the most important thing.

After one hour of brainstorming I become hungry, so it is time for dinner. Since we were invited to a birthday party in the camp, we get a delicious dinner there. At around 11PM it is time for us to go back to our tents. There, the comrades from EOD are still awake, but I am so tired, I go straight to bed away. At around 6am I wake up to the sound of soldiers running around. I ask a comrade from EOD, what the matter is. He is quite bewildered and asks me, if I don't know what happened last night? I am awake right away. Apparently, our camp was attacked with rockets and two of them hit the ground not far from our tent but didn't detonate. I think for myself: "Wow, you really have been lucky!" Less than 100m from our tent there are two unexploded rockets. Normally, those rockets, called Rocket Propelled Grenades or RPG, are fired by handheld devices. However, the Taliban build makeshift launchpads out of stones and just fire them manually. This way, they can't aim properly and the grenades just fly in the approximate direction, which is good for us. I need to get my head around what just happened, so I put on my clothes. For the comrades around here, a rocket attack is something completely normal. For me it was the first attack of my deployment and I slept right through it.

Back at Camp Marmal, we do a thorough assessment of our collected information and data from Kunduz, so we can fill our archive database with it. I forget about the incident with the rocket attack quite fast, since there is a new task for us: the inaugural visit of the new German General of RC North, General Fritz, with Atta Mohammad Noor, the Governor of the Balch province.

The Tadjik Atta was appointed his position in the autumn of 2004 by state president Hamid Karzai and as such is in an ongoing power struggle with Uzbek General Abdul Raschid Dostum.

Before the soviet invasion, Dostum was a teacher at first, then a mujahedin, as the "holy warriors" are called, and later the commander of the northern alliance in Afghanistan, which was military and political alliance against the Taliban. The day of his inauguration I drive to the side entrance of the German Headquarter ISAF. One has to imagine this like a maximum security facility, where you can only enter if you have the necessary clearance and a chip to open the door. The comrades working there only go out for lunch and sleeping, otherwise they spend their whole day there, since the whole command of the ISAF troops is there. The work there takes place behind computer monitors and desks as opposed to the other comrades working outside the camp.

The General and his three bodyguards will be in one of our three vehicles, the rest of us in the other two cars. The bodyguards protect him day and night against any danger.

I approach the bodyguards and they explain today's schedule to me. About 20 minutes later the

General and his bodyguards emerge from the building with Tobias and get into the cars. Tobias drives with me and two additional soldiers from the media division assigned to secure the parameter. We drive out of the camp and down the road to Mazar-e-Sharif until we reach the home of the Governor. The whole compound as well as the main gate is highly secured. After passing the gate, we drive towards a magnificent palace, where the General and his entourage exit the car.

We park the vehicles across the main entrance where we dropped off the VIPs. We leave our weapons secured and not visible in the cars. I know it sounds strange, but in this country, the rules of hospitality prohibit entering the house of your host while being armed. During our visit, the protection is in the hands of the host, so we are secured by the governor's bodyguards. They lead us into a waiting hall where refreshments are waiting for us while the General and the Governor proceed further to another room, where the meeting will take place. After the official meeting, we are all invited to dinner. I am completely dumbfounded about all the tasty looking food that is served. Everything you can imagine is placed on the table. Lamb, various rice dishes, fruits and vegetables as well as many other things I have never seen before. It is all very delicious and more than any of us can eat.

After dinner, we are invited to take a look around the palace. I was absolutely astonished by so much wealth. We see a lot of gorgeous paintings, especially a large-scale painting of the governor himself is standing out rather prominently. The staff is running around with fresh fruit plates and delicious pastries. After having seen parts of the palace, they lead us to the garden, which is arranged in European baroque style with fountains, statuaries and ponds, where koi carps swim in lazy circles. Before leaving this place, the VIPs enjoy a cup of freshly brewed coffee together in this amazing garden. Until this day, I never had the privilege to experience something like that or even had any idea how such a reception actually looks like. It was quite impressive for me to be a part of it and actually getting to meet the Governor in person.

It is dark when we head back to the camp. This visit has been astonishing for me and it won't be my last visit to this place.

Getting to know Governor Atta Noor in person

17. Charity for a orphanage

Not far away from camp MARMAL there is the orphanage and children asylum of MAZAR-I-SHARIF. In order to understand the following recollection it is necessary to know about the, let's put it mildly, "special" laws regarding the lawful punishment of afghan women. If a mother in Afghanistan is convicted for a crime, the child has to accompany her to prison. Don't think even for a second that the law enforcement or the prisons are somehow adjusted to this type of situation. They are absolutely not. The child loses its entire freedom as well as it has to face the same horrible consequences and conditions as its mother. It loses every chance for proper care, joy and education.

In order to somehow bring some relief to these miserable children, the TAA team in cooperation with the German Federal Police who were training Afghan Police Forces those days, established the contact to the director of the main prison in MAZAR in order to find a solution for these kids. The plan of the project was finding a possibility and convincing the authorities to accommodate the children in the orphanage during the week, where they would get at least some of the care and recognition they are so much in need of as well as some basic preschool education comparable with what we have back home in the last year of the kindergarten. That way, the children could at least escape the isolation from the rest of the world from Monday till Friday. To achieve this possibility in general, first of all the infrastructure of the orphanage had to be improved by renovating and repairing the buildings and rooms. Furthermore, a shuttle bus service had to be established in order to guarantee the transport of the children to their imprisoned mothers on Fridays and back in order to maintain the bonds between mother and child.

Already during my first visit to the asylum I was witnessing a lot of German soldiers working there on the renovation of the rest rooms and the dining room. To make the shuttle bus service happen, a lot of money still had to be allocated which was not an easy task in such a poor country. But hope dies at last, and as optimistic as we were those days, we started right away to solve this issue with a lot of motivation. We approached the German Military Radio Channel "Radio Andernach" and initiated a mission wide announcement for a donation of money for this humanitarian cause. We organized a rally in form of a donation marathon with food stands and a lottery along with it. The radio channel was advertising it down the ranks. The rally was planned to last from Friday till Sunday. All the income of the sponsored runners, the lottery tickets and the sold food would go directly into the donation account.

Eight days after the first announcement our donation rally started. I, along with our IEB team, was doing the 15 kilometers in just one hour. After the 3 days of donation rallying activities we collected

4500 US-Dollars. It was not the complete amount that was needed but the rest that was missing for buying the bus was generously donated by Nino, the boss of our "Marke Tender" store. Furthermore, the families of the German soldiers back home donated and sent clothes and toys which were packed in a steel box tagged for the individual child. All in all, it was a very successful initiative.

The bus, along with a driver we hired, was handed over to the orphanage only a few weeks later. I will never forget the look in the eyes of the children when they saw the bus for the first time. It reminded me that this is one of the reasons why we were there as well; to bring a better life to these war-torn children and to pave the way for a better future for them.

Visit at the children`s home in Mazar e Sharif

They like to be photographed with us

Heike is surrounded by Afghan youth

The slightly different one drives a car

18. Meeting again after 13 years

Two days after meeting governor NOOR at his palace I had to bring over a folder to the Generals front office. I leave mine and pass the post office on my way to the class 1 security area of the HQ. Due to me not having one of these fancy chip cards for access, I have to show the security guys at the entrance my accreditation which is authorizing me for access. I then head to the building where the General is located at, when someone is approaching me covered from my view by the blindingly bright sun. Almost to late I recognize the person walking over to me. It's my former company commander from my times in NAGOLD. A Major back then, now a Colonel, is passing by and I address him.

"Good morning Colonel! Remember me?"

He seems quite confused and has a look on the name tag of my field uniform. Then he says: "Meyer. You haven't changed much. I am a little bit in a rush right now but pay me a visit in Camp Mike Spann. That's where I stay."
I can't stop wondering. It's really my former commander standing right in front of me in a mission environment in Afghanistan 13 years after we met the last time. He leaves and I proceed with delivering the folder to the Generals front office. After-

wards I go back to my office and report to my Lieutenant Colonel what just happened. He just replied: "Well we are going to have our introduction visit to Camp Spann next week. Would you like to join?" I look at him with a fat smile on my face and say: "Is the pope a catholic? Of course, I want to join you! Actually, who else should drive you there if not me?"

On the following Saturday 26th of June, we drive to Camp Mike Spann which is located on the opposite side of MAZAR in order to introduce my Lieutenant Colonel to Colonel B. The joy of meeting again with the Colonel was immense. Camp Spann is US-forces field camp attached to the Shaheen Baracks of the 209th Corps of the Afghan National Army (ANA). The German forces stationed in this camp were assigned to advise the corps under the command of Major General Zalmai WESA in military operations and evaluate their progress.

When we arrived at the camp we parked on the official parking lot and walked for quite a while to the accommodation of the Colonel. Due to him still being occupied in a meeting we had to wait in a room where the soldiers had prepared something like a relax area with a TV, a coffee bar and cozy couches. Some of the guys were having a break and we talked about their duties over here.

After the meeting marathon the Colonel finally finds the time to receive us for a chat. We sit down in his office and talk in a relaxed atmosphere about the situation in the camp and the main goals he is responsible for to achieve. Before we leave I ask him if we could have a picture together. He laughs and agrees, of course. I am grinning and remember that he had always been this fun loving guy. After the photo shoot the Lieutenant Colonel has a look on his watch and realises that we really have to get some lunch. This time we are blessed with having lunch at our fellow American soldiers' canteen in Camp Spann and I am serious when I say it was a revelation compared to what we have known so far.

Visiting Colonel B. in camp Spann

19. The Blue Moque of Mazar-E-Sharif

I t is a Monday morning, 0730 hours. I am already in my office preparing the information documents and the vehicle for the upcoming visit to the "Blue Mosque" in MES. It is not just about visiting an important religious site. We are going to meet with the three highest religious representatives of the BALKH region there in order to introduce us and our mission goals. It's definitely time that our team becomes complete. At some point, it gets more and more stressful to organise everything all on my own. At 1000 hours we get started and pass by the interpreters' offices to pick up one of them who has been assigned to us for this trip.

Arriving at the mosque we are welcomed by some security personnel followed by the procedure of taking off our boots and placing them into a designated wooden shelf outside before we can enter. In that moment I am praying for my boots still to be at their spot when we will be done here. The first steps into the front yard of the mosque´s areal are turning in to a moment of astonishment.

Floors, roofs and walls are covered with blue, turquoise and white marble and its colours are illuminated brightly by the morning sun. An impression like from "1001 nights". Just beautiful. Next to the entrance of the prayer's hall, where access is only granted to Muslims, there is a door leading to a reception room, where three typically Afghan style dressed men are already waiting for us. These are Hadiji Atiqullah ANSARI, Director of the Blue Mosque, Hadiji HAYATULAH, Director for Hadj related issues for whole northern Afghanistan, and Hadiji ZALMAI, tribal elder of the Pashtun. All of them wear different head gear according to their ethnical background and their position within the Afghan society.

Entrance to the Blue Mosque

After the typical welcome phrases by the Lieuten-ant Colonel and some personal greetings from the Commander which he had to pass over, the repre-sentatives reply by their typical greetings adding how nice it is to meet again with ISAF officials ex-pecting us to fulfill the promises made in the past. A quite harsh and not very kind way to approach your guests, I personally think, but I will learn eventually, that he has good reasons for his rudeness which was caused by disappointment.

For more than a year no contact has been maintained by ISAF nor have scheduled appointments been attended by mission personnel. It took a lot of discussion to convince them of our reliability and integrity, but in the end all issues were addressed and further steps for cooperation agreed on. All in all, an important success. Only the tribal leader seems to be very distanced during the meeting. While the other two speak almost without any break, he is just patiently listening and observing us very intensely. During the discussion, I understand how important wording in general is over here. It is quite a serious thing. Everything you say is taken for granted and the worst thing you can do is to promise something you cannot keep.

At some point we go into detail of the various agenda points. An essential project which was discussed already a lot in the past but has never really been taken care of, are the irrigation ditches in the area of BALKH and KHOLM. This is the key word for the tribal elder. Suddenly he gets involved and takes over the conversation. He is mentioning that he has 1500 men only waiting for his order, ready to start the work if only the help funds were finally disbursed. And that is actually the point my boss was waiting for the whole time.

He tries to explain to the men that this money and the 1500 men by themselves cannot be the solution.

This project as well as all the others with the assistance of ISAF and/or civil charity organisations can only provide an initial boost, which has to be taken over by the Afghan authorities, with continuous ISAF support in the background. To bring this topic to an end, at least for today, my boss offers to report the issue to the commander right after being back to the camp and invites the three men on behalf of the commander to a follow-on meeting at to our base.

It has gotten late and we leave the representatives, heading in the direction of our boots and thank God, they are still there. On the way back, I revise the discussion in my mind accompanied by the scenes of the people in the streets of this ancient city. You cannot compare such a ride with a city bus tour through Munich. You see the people and you see the long way this country still has to go. They are the same thoughts I had while being in KUNDUZ. A lot of good and meaningful projects were realized, but you can tell by so many unsolved issues that it will take a long time until this country will be able to breathe freely and be satisfied.

The front yard of the blue mosque

20. Visit by the commander

After the visit of the Blue Mosque I (alone, of course) have to transfer all the gathered information, POCs and observations into our archive.

Our data base gets filled more and more and it's interesting to see which people I have already met during my time here in MES. Today we will be visited by the commander of our national unit in MAYEN, Germany, in order for him to get an impression of our actual duties and performance over here. Until now, he only got informed via mail or phone conversations. He is expected to arrive at around 1100 hours, which gives me some time to accomplish some tasks for the day.

While I am doing some random admin stuff which is unavoidable in the modern mission environment, the door of my office opens and my boss, together with the Commander, Colonel R. are coming right to me. I immediately stand up and raise my hand for a military salute. The Colonel makes quite a pleasant impression like it used to be back home. After a short greeting, the two officers sit down, I get them some refreshments and pass my boss our projects folder. To keep the proper distance, I leave the office and go to meet with Sven for coffee. When I am back, the Lieutenant Colonel is still busy to brief Colonel R., so I sneak to my desk and keep on doing my amazingly thrilling administrative tasks.

I don't catch most of the discussion, but I can observe that the Colonel is listening intensively. When they are done, he comes over and tells me with this typical smile on his face that, according to his impression, we did a very good job so far and that my boss can praise the lord for having such a professional and reliable NCO by his side who is both supporting and motivating him in so many cases. He gives me his hand and adds that whenever I will be back to Germany I should come around for a debriefing, because he wouldn't be able to do it during this trip, since he had to visit a few other branches and sections. Honoured by such words, I say farewell to the Colonel and continue my work freshly motivated. Not expecting something could top the Colonels visit today, there is another surprise waiting for me.

In the afternoon I receive the approval for extending my assignment here till the end of the 23rd mission contingent which I am really happy about, since this means that I will stay as long as my boss and that we will leave this place together. The only thing still missing is the approval for our request for support by additional personnel. Having an additional guy helping us with our responsibilities for the three main locations would really help us out.

21. Driving tot he Teacher Training Center

This morning, a Lieutenant Colonel from the department of Target Group Analysis (TAA) came to our office, asking if it would be possible to get a vehicle and a driver from us at around 10 o'clock. The destination would be the training center for future teachers in Mazar-e-Sharif.

I could tell him right away that we had no additional tasks outside the camp for today. In order to get exact information regarding the routing, I go over to the office of the TAA and discuss the timetable with Heike, an Ensign and officer in charge of the planned field trip. Since we also need two additional passengers acting as a security detail, I also pay a visit to Sven to get two of his comrades from PsyOps.

Shortly after ten o'clock we start with our twenty-minute drive to the school. Arriving at the training center, we park our cars right in front of the school and start to establish a security perimeter. It is the job of our security personal to a ensure our safety form attacks during our stay and the discussion at the school. While we secure the courtyard, some of the pupils already have end of terms and leave the building. The young female students are wearing mostly European clothes like jeans and blouses, but right before leaving the courtyard, they all put on a burka, so the western clothing won't show.

This was rather surprising for me. Nothing I would have expected in a country so proud of their traditions. After one and a half hours our conversation is over and we arrange a new date for the next meeting. We all meet in the courtyard and drive back to the camp. I found out later that those students had begun a project called "Learn better – understand better" so they would be able – when being a teacher themselves - to teach their respective subjects to their students. I think it is quite a challenge to teach a child from country where most of their parents are illiterate. But on the other hand, most parents value the education of their children, since they can learn a bit for themselves.

I have seen quite often that children read the contents of the ISAF newspaper to their parents who can't read. I also realized that the parents depend on their children very much, for example when working in the fields, to fetch water from the nearby river or to look after the goats. Those kids really have a challenging childhood, different to our own children at home. Back at the camp, I refuel the car and then drive over to the car wash, nicknamed "Mr. Wash".

The Afghan national working there washes all or cars and tanks in the camp with simply a hose, daily from Sunday till Thursday. Next stop is the ATU, also a nickname for our car repair shop. There I do all the necessary maintenance work, but when needed there are specialists who can help with repairs. After that, my car is ready and safe to be used again. After the maintenance work I go back to the office to see if there are any new tasks. Arriving there I see my boss is about to leave so I wish him a pleasant day, something I always say.

Students leaving the Teacher Training Cente

22. Religious dignitaries at Camp Marmal

After our new Commander issued an invitation to visit Camp Marmal, many religious dignitaries of both Sunnites and Shiites as well as the governor of the Balkh province, Atta Mohammed Noor, and the dean of the University of Masar-e-Sharif followed this invitation. My task is to fetch the people from the guest list at the main gate and to accompany them to the entrance of the security parameter, where the Commander welcomes his guests. After that I show the drivers to the nearby tent, where they can stay until the meeting is over. It all goes according to plan and it is done within one hour. I take care of our guests, offering some snacks like nuts and pieces of watermelon as well as cold drinks.

Next to the tent is a bazar, an Afghan market, originally intended for the soldiers of the camp, but our curious guests quickly find something they want to buy.

Meanwhile, our Commander and the religious dignitaries also get some snacks. One of the main topics of the meeting is the Ramadan and the planned Ramadan cards for our soldiers. As mentioned before, those cards are supposed to explain the soldiers the right behavior during this important month. The content of this cards is explained to our guests, and, as I found out later, was approved by all of them.

Ramadan in Afghanistan is something quite extraordinary, especially if one has the opportunity to be invited for dinner.

I was lucky to attend such a dinner as companion of an officer at the house of Jawid Barrad and his family. He was a candidate at the election of the parliament in 2010. You can't imagine the ridiculous amounts of food that were served, not only for family but also for relatives, friends and guests. I wouldn't have stood out if it hadn't been for my uniform. But wearing it, I could clearly be recognized as a foreigner, although my hosts never made me feel like one.

The Afghan food mainly included rice, lamb and goat milk curt, all freshly prepared. The thought of it makes me crave this kind of food again, it is really delicious.

Taking care of the drivers

Election candidate Jawid Barrad

Afghan food, traditionally eaten without cutlery

23. The newbies are coming

It is July 15th, 9 o'clock in the morning. I am sitting in my office, preparing the driving assignments, when Sven enters and asks me if I had forgotten something. Since I couldn't think of a task that I might have forgotten, I just ask him: "Should I?" He starts laughing and responds: "What about the aircraft from Termez?" Looking at the clock makes me jump off my seat. In less than ten minutes the new comrades from Germany will arrive via aircraft from Termez, including a Sergeant who will work at our office. And here I am, still sitting in the office!

"Get moving, you can drive with me!" Sven isn't exactly renowned for being nice, but at least you know quite fast, what he wants. At that moment, my phone rings. It is someone from the translator and interpreter department, asking if we forgot to pick up our new translator, since he is waiting at the airport. About ten minutes later we arrive at the airfield, normally full of people and equipment waiting to be picked up. Now, there is only a single backpack and next to it Master Sergeant N., our new translator. I walk over to welcome him. As for every new arrival, he has to do the in-processing, but first, we carry his luggage over to the container, where the other translators sleep as well. The soldier, a Staff Sergeant, who is supposed to help me with my tasks will arrive in four weeks. Then our staff at the IEB will have all its needed personal.

Those four weeks go by fast and this time Sven doesn't need to remind me to pick him up from the airfield. Nabil and I drive down to the airfield and wait until the plane arrives. When new soldiers arrive, it is always a good opportunity for getting new information since there are almost always the same people picking up the new arrivals from the airport. So we always exchange the new information between the different units. The newbies, we call them "Tappsis", exit the shuttle bus behind the departure lounge. We recognize our new comrade immediately, since he is already waiting next to his luggage. We go over to him and welcome him to Mazar-e-Sharif.

After the welcome we drive to his container, where he will live during his time in MeS; it is also my container. The tour around the camp will take place later, because I have some tasks that I need to finish, so there is no time for it. But he uses the time to stow all his equipment.

Stephan and Nabil, my teammates at IEB

24. Getting acquainted with medical personal during flight

After a short 9-day vacation I am sitting at the airport of Cologne again, waiting to check in for my flight o Afghanistan. Like every time I fly to Afghanistan, I am sitting in the waiting room, watching as it fills with soldiers and civilians about to fly with the same aircraft.

Normally, you don't know anyone before departure, but during the 6-8 hour flight to Termez you get to talk to some of them. After the boarding I sit next to two women and three men, who all go to Mazar-e-Sharif as well. So we get to know each other better. Levka, Sonja, Baschir, Masud and Christian are all students of medicine at the University Witten/Hagen who participate in the "Medical Exchange Program Mazar". Their goal is to educate other students in Afghanistan with four workshops, from emergency medicine over vein-puncturing to internal medicine for women at the local hospital of Mazar-e-Sharif.

I am listening to them intensively and offer them a chance to visit our Camp Marmal, so they can see how our army medical center works. They are quite excited about this, so we exchange our phone numbers in order to arrange a meeting. Due to our conversation the long flight hours go by fast and we arrive at Termez. During the time waiting for the flight to MeS, I take care of them, since they are not familiar with the procedures at the Termez airport. At 7 am we finally board the Transall to Mazar-e-Sharif. Arriving at MeS, we say goodbye for now and I promise them to arrange a visit at the camp.

After landing in MeS, I am happy to see Stefan and Nabil waiting for me. We take a small detour to my housing container before we drive to the office, where I report back for duty to my boss. I tell him the news from Germany and of course about the students I invited to our camp. Since it is not that easy to get them in here, I ask my boss to get the permission from the Commander. After receiving the permission, I start planning the program for the students, including a visit at the field hospital and at PsyOps, an interview at Radio Andernach, a visit at the "marketender" of the Norwegian forces and at the Afghan bazaar inside the camp. After that I intent to walk around the base, have lunch and coffee and finally visit my own unit. After getting the go from my boss, I arrange the time and date with Levka. She also invites us to one of the workshops, so we can see how things work at the hospital.

25. A day in the camp with five students

It is 9 o'clock in the morning in Afghanistan, the sun is shining, it is quite hot already and I prepare everything to fetch our visitors with two of our vehicles from the hospital in Mazar-e-Sharif. Before driving back, a small tour around the hospital is planned to see the students at work. Stefan and Nabil take the first car, my boss and I drive the second one. This way, we can take all the students safely to the camp. Our meeting at the hospital is scheduled for 10:15 local time. We start at the camp at 09:30 local time, this time along the desert route on the right side of the camp. Since this route is not frequently used, we arrive at MeS shortly after. Arriving at the hospital, we are welcomed by Baschir, the founder of this project. We already know each other from our flight together, so I introduce my comrades to him. After that we go to the training room, where mostly female afghan students learn suturing by using pig foots. I am quite impressed by how skilled they close up the wounds. While watching, they explain to us the different techniques to close wounds, a fascinating topic that we will definitely not forget.

After cleaning up the room, all of us have our photo taken together with the professor of the clinic and the students. Then we drive back to Camp Marmal where we go with our guests to the canteen for lunch. After lunch, we proceed to Radio Andernach, where the students are interviewed. Due to our busy schedule we go to the field hospital next, where the students learn about the different injuries occurring here and how to treat them. The patients are not only German soldiers, but Afghan soldiers and policemen as well as civilians. The next stop is the Norwegian part of the camp, where we visit the "Marketender" shop and the different recreational opportunities there, like a small supermarket selling chocolate and cigarettes. Even a pizza parlor exists. The students take some pictures from the roof of the "Marketender", and even some funny ones of themselves.

After that we continue our tour around the camp so the students can see how big the camp actually is and what installations there are. Twenty minutes later we reach PsyOps where I show our guests the combat camera team "EKT" and what the job of this three men unit is: one who conducts interviews, one camera operator who films everything and is also responsible for the weapons on board their vehicle and one satcom Sergeant who broadcasts everything worldwide and who also acts as the driver and principle photographer. This three men unit is very versatile and resourceful, since they have to operate under harsh conditions in a foreign country. Their work is vital for the planning, executing and debriefing of operations. They analyse the current situation and make decisions about the further course of action against the Taliban possible. They also do reconnaissance work for new safe routes and establish a so called "routebook". This means finding new evacuation routes as well as potentially dangerous waypoints, so that the leaders have a clear picture of the potential threats. It is similar to a reconnaissance group, just instead of intel, they capture all this on camera.

Supporting the PR crew is also part of their job. The EKT contribute articles for several news feeds, so people at home know what is going on in Afghanistan. We also visit the different parts of Psy-Ops, Video, Audio and Print media. They are used to distribute information to different target groups, for example flyers and radio for the north of Afghanistan, so that the public can be informed easily about the Taliban with pictures. This way, the locals can inform ISAF, if they see one of the Taliban. They also do this for other countries as well as all of Afghanistan.

The main benefit is, that the military can act faster to help keep the people safe and without fear.

Our guests are quite impressed by all the effort the Bundeswehr puts into this mission, especially since they are allowed to see all this live. Their opinion about our mission also changes for the better, since they now have more information.

The time went by quickly, so we skip visiting the IEB and go directly to Radio Andernach, where we are already expected.

The editor, Lieutenant F. is waiting for us and gives the students a warm welcome. They proceed to visiting all the different parts of the radio station.

You can get greetings from home and also the music you like. I got a message from my son once, that was a great feeling, as if my family was here.

While the students do their interview, Nabil and I play some table kicker and I win despite not having played for a long time. One and a half hours later, the visit is over. They are very impressed about what they saw and the work we are doing. After thanking us for the great day, they drive back to Mazar-e-Sharif. But we will see each other again on the day the leave for Germany again. So, we say goodbye for now and drive back to the camp. It was quite a fun day, showing those young people our side of this mission that is not so well known back in Germany.

Fotoshoot on the roof of the Maketender

A visit at Radio Andernach

SatCom Sergeant working

Nabil playing kicker at Radio Andernach in the camp

26. Afghanistan-Projekt „no más fonteras"

I t is October 14th, in the morning around 8:00
a.m. I'm in the office and going about my duties when Tobias comes into the office and we
start our daily morning update. Item 1 is about to
be a surprise. On 16th and 17th October, we'll get a
visit from an artist, philosopher and cultural activist named Batuz. What I do not know at that time
are the successes of this American artist. He has already carried out several projects and has thus
gained great international attention. Now he plans
to stay in Afghanistan for about three weeks and to
pitch his tents in Camp Marmal during this time.
From here he would like to visit Kabul (کابل), Herat
(هرات) and the province of Bamian. In addition, he
would like to repeat a project that he already carried out in 2002 with Polish and German soldiers in
a spectacular action in the middle of the border
river Neisse, but this time the scene will be in northern Afghanistan. The project should symbolically
show that borders can be overcome, even after cen-
turies of suffering. At the end of June 2009, soldiers
of 37 DEU Armoured Infantry Brigade already
formed a human chain with broad public and media participation in Frankenberg, Germany - for
many a kind of dress rehearsal for a similar mani-
festation in Afghanistan. At that time, the project
required talks with the ministers of culture and
higher education as well as with the governors of

the provinces visited. Within this framework, contact with the German armed forces was also further expanded.

The Federal Minister of Defence at that time, Karl-Theodor Freiherr zu Gutenberg, had already declared his willingness to support the new project within the scope of the capabilities of the German Army in a letter to General von Kirchbach at the end of July 2010, while at the same time pointing out the difficult current situation in Afghanistan. Everyone is aware that such a project can only be successful here if it is based on the cooperation of all or at least the most important, sometimes rival groups in the country. At the beginning of the project it becomes clear that this will require a lot of persuasion. But after more than 30 years of armed conflict and economic hardship, there is a strong longing for peace and stability in Afghanistan. To promote both is the primary aim of the Batuz project. It will be my task to look after Batuz during his time in the camp and to give him all the support he needs. After the briefing, my boss Tobias will instruct me to take care of the wellbeing of Batuz. He should want for nothing; his project must be a success, no matter what. I am also supposed to give the commander both an interim and final report about the project. Now I know what to expect ... at least I think so at this point in time. Until Batuz's arrival there are still 2 days left to prepare myself. First of all, I take care of the artist's accommodation; it should not be far away from the mess hall, so it is convenient to have his daily meals. As I like to do things in a flexible way, all other preparations will only be done upon his arrival. Since I have already established all my required contacts, it will be easy for me to avoid chaos.

27. US-American artist arrives

On October 16, around 9 o'clock in the morning my boss, Nabil and I are standing with our vehicle at the "Main Gate" to pick up our guest, Batuz. He is accompanied by a former freedom fighter general, General Wasiq. Batuz is the founder of the "Société Imaginaire", a "cultural response to globalization". He is also known for his anti-wall project in Berlin in 1984, for an art project linking Germany and Poland in 2002, and finally for the project "no más fronteras "a cross-border art project in 2007.

I only really understood at a later point, that Batuz' messages to the people through his art are truly unique. At the time when I got the task, I thought to myself, "Wow, what a special and unique project here in Afghanistan". Until this point in time, I couldn't imagine anything specific about his projects, because I knew nothing about him and his work. But I can already tell that my view will change. The first installation of Batuz' gigantic work, measuring 5.50 meters x 11.30 meters, was designed with helmets of dead soldiers and was, like all his works, dedicated to peace. But I only

received this information much later, when Batuz had already arrived at the camp.

As we are standing in front of the camp gate awaiting the arrival of our visitor, I ask the question to the others, how our guest will probably influence our life on camp. Nabil and my boss hold back with their opinions and just shrug their shoulders. I, on the other hand, am curious to see who is coming. Since I already know his face from the internet, I'm just wondering, does he really look the same or has he changed a lot? And the most important thing is, what can I do to help him fulfil his dream.

Before I can think about it, our guest arrives at the gate. The driver's door opens and General Wasiq gets out of his SUV and walks around the car to help Batuz to get out. When he leaves the car and approaches to greet us, I immediately notice that he looks exactly the same as on the photo I saw a few days before.

at the gate by Nabil and me

After the welcome I load the luggage into our vehicle and ask Batuz to get in. We drive directly to his accommodation so that he can rest and freshen up after the long drive. About 1.5 hours later I pick him up for dinner and show him the mess hall where the meals are taken by all soldiers except the Americans. We enter the large mess hall and I briefly explain to him the procedure of how the food is served. With the food on our trays we walk to a table where some Hungarian comrades are already sitting and eating, and take a seat with them. During the dinner I introduce myself in more detail and explain my tasks in the IEB, because after all we are supposed to work together for a while. He listens to me with great interest and I am amazed how quickly I can establish a connection to him. I soon realize that he is a very wise man who has had to go through many difficult times in his life so far. I am all the more impressed now that he has almost always been able to achieve the goals he has set himself up until now. He is a man who, despite all the obstacles that have stood in his way, has lost nothing of his zest for life, and I find this quite impressive. And I know for sure that the next days and weeks will be very interesting.

The very next morning we sit together again and discuss the procedure and the tasks for today. I quickly notice that Batuz is a perfectionist. He immediately makes detailed notes of everything that comes to his mind and later elaborates on them in detail. This is how he intends to get people excited about the project and to get them on our side. No matter if it is a German, a Polish or a Norwegian comrade. It is important in this first phase that we get as many helpers and supporters as possible not only from our own ranks but also from the Afghan staff. The latter are particularly important, since the artistic performance is primarily intended to draw attention to the freedom of the country and its people. To make this project public on camp we first create a draft poster in different languages, such as English, German and Dari, that will serve as an advertisement for the project on November 4, 2010. This poster will then be placed at all prominent points on camp so that as many comrades as possible can see it. A poster will be placed everywhere where comrades from all nations stay and spend their time together. In his book, Batuz shows me his previous works of art, which impressively present the theme "No màs fronteras", in English: "No more boundaries", and how he would like to connect this theme with the Afghanistan project. As background image for the poster we take a picture from his book, which depicts the border on a mountain slope and a boundary on a rough surface. It should symbolically reflect the theme "overcoming borders".

Once the initial steps of the project have been launched, I am now trying to make a sketch of the area with the help of our construction office. With the office's information, we will later draw the border lines on the Afghan soil. After scanning, a large plotter will be used to print out the plan, which will help us to measure the border line. In addition to the plan, we will also need measuring tapes, parcel string, fluorescent spray and black cloths for the participants, which will then represent the border. I can get most of it from our hardware store. We will have one of our Afghan language mediators get the cloths from the Afghan market. All that is missing now are people who will help us with the preparation and implementation of the project Afghanistan. However, this will prove to be more difficult than initially thought. It is not so easy to raise interest or get support for the project, because many people only smile about it and obviously have not understood the purpose of this project at all.

One evening, Batuz and I are sitting together in the reception area of our bar, having a drink and talking about this and that when a Hungarian captain walks up to us and sits down beside us on the sofa. He greets us in a friendly manner and although we seem to be somewhat separated by the language, Batuz immediately starts a conversation with the Hungarian captain in his native language. The spell is broken immediately and there is no more talk of distance; at least not between the captain and Batuz, because with the best will in the world I could not understand a word they were saying. Shortly after the conversation is over, he tells me that the Hungarian captain will provide us five of his comrades to support the preparations.

And with that we have our advance party together: Stephan, Nabil, myself, the five Hungarian comrades and the artist. In total we are now nine people who can get the project off the ground. And from the construction office we also get the OK that one comrade can help and support us, at least in the beginning. And with that the foundation stone has been laid; what is still missing is the venue. In order to generate sufficient interest from the media, ideal would be a place that would attract as much attention as possible. In any case, such a place should be located outside the camp, although it is quite obvious that this is not feasible in this war-torn region. Due to the security situation, Batuz's wish to set up a human chain at the foothills of the Hindu Kush is therefore denied. In a personal conversation with Major General F., he is informed that the planned project can only take place within the camp, and only with the Afghan staff there. When Batuz returns from this conversation with the general, he is slightly uncertain whether the Afghanistan project can create enough media interest at all. He had hoped for a large contingent of international media representatives to publicize the pictures to the world so that the message of peace would be spread as widely as possible. But being restricted to the camp, this is no longer possible.

He seems to be quite disappointed about it and I can totally understand that, because when you have such a big idea in your head, it is not always easy to reduce it to a smaller scale. But on the other hand, I also understand our leadership, because after all they are responsible for the lives of the soldiers - and also for the life of Batuz. It is difficult to do justice to both sides here. I try to explain the circumstances to him and of course he also sees the need for safety of all involved. I promise him that we will nevertheless make the best of the situation. The next morning after breakfast, it is beautiful weather; we meet in front of the shelter, that's what we call the containers in which we live. The view of the Hindu Kush is once again breathtaking. High mountains, which today look completely different than yesterday.

The day before there was still a light fog over the mountain range and today they shine like pure gold. You could think it was golden sand, but it in reality it is rock. When I arrive at the shelter, Batuz is already sitting over his documents and is busy making notes about which tasks still have to be done; from buying the fabric, to completing telephone calls with all sorts of people. I'm always fascinated anew about what far-reaching contacts this man has. It is interesting to listen to him when he begins to tell where and on what occasion he met this or that person, especially in the military.

And just as much as I enjoy listening to him, I notice that it is good for him to talk about it, too. In the meantime, Stephan and Nabil are in the process of getting the tools together for later. Today we will first try to locate a suitable place for the human chain on 4th November. For this purpose, we drive to the outer area of the camp, where the first construction work for the resettlement of the Americans from Baghdad, the capital of Iraq, to Mazar-e Sharif are already in full swing. From there you have a good view of the Hindu Kush which will appear later in the background of the photos. But it will still take some time until we have found the optimal place because Batuz is very picky which becomes very clear after 1.5 hours of searching.

Helmets for Peace, courtesy of artist Batuz

Preparation for day X with Hungarian support

But we don't give up and finally we find what we are looking for. We immediately mark the place with the barrier tape we brought along, so that the boundaries are clearly visible. So now that we have found a location, we can start with measuring and marking the imaginary border line during the next days, on which the people should form a human chain to demonstrate how peace can connect.

Meanwhile day "X" is getting closer and closer.

It is now Monday, 1st November. At 9 o'clock all the support staff arrives at the square to help us with the preparations. With maps, route tape and lots of spray cans we start to draw the planned border line on the Afghan ground. Our Hungarian comrades are also on site to support us hands on. The beginning is a little bit difficult, because we don't all quite agree about where the borderline should begin. But as soon as it is clear, things start to get much better and at the end of the first day you can even see where our efforts are leading to. At the end of the second day, our work is accomplished and I think it's worth seeing. Now all that is missing are just the people who are to line up along the imaginary border line. Batuz is also visibly relieved that the work was completed so easily and that all preparations could be implemented without any further problems.

Now the day of the experiment "human chain in Afghanistan" can come. Quite satisfied with our work, we all sit together for an evening drink in the OASE and hope that the next day will be a success. And above all that enough soldiers and Afghan employees will come to form a closed human chain.

tow CH53 flying low over the camp

28. The great day oft he experiment has come

I t is November 4th 2010 in Afghanistan. The big day has come! I am in the office early this morning to make the final preparations. Stephan and Nabil have already arrived as well. We are really curious to see how many people will turn up today to take part in the human chain. Despite the initial critical attitude towards the project, in the meantime some people who want to support the project have contacted us. Even the General wanted to come by, along with his staff officers, so we can count on the support from the command group.

The last two days were hard work for all involved, even in the camp. After the preparations had been completed at our designated location, we had to cut several 100 meters of fabric rolls together with the help from the Afghan camp workers. Each soldier and Afghan employee will be given a one meter piece of cloth, which he will later wear over his head and shoulders. Now it is time to start and we will see whether all this has been worthwhile.

At 9 o'clock we have a short briefing with our boss on today's agenda. After that Nabil and I leave to pick up Batuz. Stephan and Tobias will drive directly to the square. When we arrive in front of Batuz's accommodation, I see a somewhat unusual picture. He is not as calm and quiet as I usually know him; you can clearly see his excitement. I try to calm him down by reassuring him that everything will be alright. But I don't think that's going to help much at this moment. I am quite excited and tense myself, so I can't blame him for his nervousness. Well, it was still worth a try.

Today, also other guests will come to the camp who have been invited by Batuz to attend his performance, such as General Wasiq. He brings baskets full of freshly baked white flat bread, which will later be distributed as a sign of friendship and which is supposed to represent the overcoming of boundaries between people.

When we arrive at the location, we are pleasantly surprised by what we see. Many soldiers and civilian employees as well as police officers have already arrived and more and more people are coming with the camp shuttle. Batuz welcomes the people with a megaphone, so everybody can hear what he has to say. After a short welcome speech, we start to line up the people along the marked border line and equip everyone with a black cloth. In the meantime, also the first Afghan employees arrive by bus and we immediately integrate them into the chain.

About an hour later, the human chain is finally ready for the aerial and ground photographs. The megaphone is used to communicate the tasks and to give precise instructions on how the people in the chain should be positioned, without the cloth, then with the cloth spread over their heads, then taking the right and left neighbours by the hand.

Everyone is ready but unfortunately not the helicopter that is supposed to take the aerial photos. Due to bad visibility in Termez this morning it could not take off and is therefore not available for today. But as always, where there is a will there is a way. And that's why we are now simply taking the ambulance which is on site anyway, to be ready for a possible mission. We place a cameraman in the front of the ambulance who then films from out of the roof hatch while the vehicle passes the human chain. A second photographer takes pictures from the ground.

After the first video clips and photos are taken, the flat bread comes into play. It is meant to symbolize how enemies can become friends. One breaks the bread and hands it to his neighbour. Later, they embrace each other and eat the bread together. To see these peaceful images live is very impressive, especially when you have seen the situation of the Afghans out on the streets, in the country and in the city.

At this moment all I can think about is why it can't be the same everywhere in the world; that people can work and live together without being separated by intolerance or irrational hatred. Then there would be no more wars or violence against minorities; simply living together without conflict. Is it too good to be true? Well, at least today, with this project we have made it!

At the end of the experiment, the General addresses a few words to the artist and to all those who have helped to make this project possible. Thus, another project "no más fronteras" has been successfully carried out in Afghanistan and documented for eternity. And I am inwardly happy that, despite all the big and small obstacles, the project went so smoothly.

A few days later Batuz leaves us again. He thanks me for the great support and says that he has found another friend in his life. In the hope of a reunion, he invites me to Berlin and I gladly accept his invitation. I feel very honoured to hear these words from such a motivated and successful man and I am already looking forward to taking him up on his offer.

Batuz a man who can enchant people

Breaking bread as a symbol of how enemies can become friends

Friendly embrace

Implementation of the human chain with Afghan staff and soldiers of all nations

29. Trip tot he border and port city Hairatan

Hairatan (Dari: حيرتان) is a border and port city in the north of the Balch province. It is located at an altitude of 300 metres on the southern bank of the river Amudarja, which forms the border between Afghanistan and Uzbekistan. Our mission today is to meet with the chief of the border police. We want to have a talk with him about the current security situation on the border. Later that afternoon we also plan a visit to the container terminal in Hairatan. Our route takes us via the Ring Road to Hairatan. This road is designated as "Green Route" for today; therefore it should be free of suicide bombers and IEDs, so-called booby traps. The latter are unconventional explosive and incendiary devices, which the terrorists themselves assemble from various materials. Since a new railway line is currently being built between Hairatan and Mazar-e-Sharif, it is more common for such projects to be destroyed or seriously damaged while still under construction - with the means just mentioned. This will be one of the main topics of discussion with the chief of the border police.

Our team today consists of a captain, the future Intercultural Advisor for Feyzabad, a lieutenant from Kabul with a Hungarian cameraman and soldier. Their task is to collect pictures and impressions from all over the country.

Nabil and I provide support as driver and translator. The trip to Hairatan is straightforward and without any incidents. On the way there we regularly see railway workers at work. The road to Hairatan is very good and quite new, which gives us a quiet and comfortable ride. Such conditions are an exception if you know the normal roads in Afghanistan.

Occasionally you can see farmers working on their fields, but not on good soil like in Germany. No, here the soil consists only of sand and poor undergrowth. Every now and then there is a water ditch, but mostly dried out because of the hot arid conditions.

Along the 80-kilometer-long railway line, it would be easy to hide several IEDs to destroy it. This is an issue which we want to discuss with the chief of the border police later.

After the conversation we are once again invited for lunch. This gesture is common here, the guest always gets something to eat and drink. Opposite the border control building there is a pergola which is completely overgrown with vines. Under it there is a big table with two long benches where two border guards are setting up the table. The beverage cans are iced and stand next to two oval plates with peppers, tomato slices, cucumber rings, and pepperoni and with parsley on top. Beside this, there are two huge plates with Palau, a dish with rice mixed with raisins, carrots and mutton, chicken or beef and fresh goats' curd cheese. Every time I am invited for a meal, it is another treat for me. Although the national dish should always taste the same, there is a certain difference in the taste. But what never changes is the openness and warmth of our hosts.

For the Captain, this is his first trip as an intercultural advisor since he arrived in Afghanistan 10 days ago. He is very surprised by the hospitality and later thanks the Chief of Police on behalf of all of us. After lunch we drive to the container terminal where the containers are currently being loaded onto trucks to be further transported into the centre of the country, until the railway line from Hairatan to Mazar-e-Sharif is completed.

For the most part, timber and other building materials are transported into the country. The transfer from rail to road is not as advanced as at home, as a lot of manpower and old equipment is still used. Again, proof of how much this country has a lot of catching up to do in terms of infrastructure. On the way back to the camp, we see numerous small construction sites along the future railway line, where diligent work is also being carried out. Not far from Camp Marmal the final station is already taking shape.

Uzbekistan border crossing to Afghanistan Hairatan

"Welcome to Afghanistan"

30. First visit tot he OCCR headqzarters

On the way back from the second meeting with the director of the Blue Mosque, Hadji Atiqullah Ansari, Tobias says that we still have enough time until our next appointment at the university. Therefore, we would have time to make the initial visit to the head of the department "OCCR", Operation Coordination Center Regional.

The OCCR department is a link between the Afghan Army and the German ISAF command which enables joint planning activities and operations against the insurgent groups. I'm driving with our car on the ring road around MES towards the OCCR headquarters in the Shadian Road. On the way there, I notice that there are many more Afghan soldiers and police officers about. They stand at the roadsides with their pickups, monitoring the crossroads and the entrance roads towards the city centre. Immediately I have a bad feeling in my stomach and I ask myself what is going on now? Only a few minutes later at OCCR I find out that there is another suicide bomber in a white Toyota heading in the direction of the ANA camp to carry out an attack. Luckily, we have just come from this street where the alleged suicide bomber is suspected. However, it will be difficult for the comrades to find this man on the road, because in and around MES there are hundreds of white Toyotas driving around. I have just overtaken some of these cars myself a few minutes earlier on the way here.

We are told that the suspect is probably a young man about twenty years old, who is supposed to be driving around in a white Toyota loaded with explosives to carry out the attack against the ANA camp. When I hear this, I realize again that we are not as safe as one could sometimes easily think because of the relatively peaceful life in the camp. But compared with our comrades in the military vehicles, we have one advantage as we drive a civilian and well armoured car, and you don't stand out as much as you would do with a military off-road vehicle.

Concerning suicide attacks, you learn during the pre-deployment training to pay attention to the typical signs of a suicide bomber. For example, they are supposedly mostly alone in the car; the windows are not visible from the back and the side in order for the explosives not to be detected. In addition, one should pay attention to the yellow canisters which could be filled with explosives. But in reality, the guys here are drive around in such well-prepared cars that you can't see if it is a suicide bomber or not. In the time I've been stationed in MES, we've already had several suicide bomber warnings. One of them concerned a ten-year-old boy who was allegedly waiting in the city for potential targets with a belt of explosives. Now find a boy of that age who doesn't look like he's wearing an explosive belt; and this in a city where thousands of children and young people live!

Anyway, today we have arrived safely at the OCCR and got to know the whole German team and their tasks. The team consists of five comrades, two of whom, like me, are also reservists. Thorsten, Klaus, Marc-André and Alex are responsible for keeping the communication and information exchange with the Regional Command up to date. To this end, more than three dozen Afghan staff officers and police commanders meet every day with the German team and an American colleague for a briefing. During the meeting, each side presents the incidents that have occurred in their respective units since the previous day and the security-related information they have gathered since then.

From the German side, Thorsten presents the latest information to the General and his staff in the evening update. In short, one can say: Listen, keep in touch, exchange information. These are the main points of the OCCR. I once had the opportunity to look at such a review of the last 24 hours, called a "situation report", and learned what kind of data is actually collected. It is information about attacks on ISAF troops, convoys under fire and shootings between the local army and insurgents. There was also talk about something called "troops in contact", which deals with known confrontations between units of the International Security Assistance Force and those who want to fight them. However, details about these encounters are not yet fully available.

Klaus explains that this is pretty much how it always is. It is often not possible to say exactly which troops are involved in combat and to which extent, so there is no other choice than to wait for further information. All in all, I always find it interesting to find out what other comrades do and which risks they face during their deployment.

The team, also known as the liaison element, like us, belongs to a very small part of the force which can move and drive around freely in the city and the surrounding area in order to gain insights into everyday life in Afghanistan. The visit to the OCCR team is drawing to a close, and after 1.5 hours we drive back to the camp in order to write a report about this morning's events in the office. It was nice and very informative to have met the guys.

Marc-André is always up for a joke

Alex, not only a comrade, but a good friend

31. Viait oft he Gouvernor of Samangan

Samangan (سمنگان) is a province in northern Afghanistan. It borders the provinces of Balkh, Kunduz (کندوز), Baghlan (بغلان), and Sar-e Pul (سرپل). The capital of the province is called Aybak. It is a very fertile and productive area which becomes apparent from the extensive orchards that are planted here. Besides fruits, raisins, dried fruit and honey, Afghanistan also produces agricultural products such as saffron, rose and walnut oil. Silk material and jewellery are also part of the trade goods. The province of Samangan is renowned for its fruit production; so on the way there we stop at a pomegranate plantation which is located by a river.

Accompanying us are Nabil, Stephan, Henning, Evelin and a captain from the headquarters' staff as our security support. This is something different for him than just sitting at his desk and seeing the inside of the camp. We pick some ripe pomegranates from a pomegranate tree by the roadside and eat them right there, just like the Afghans do. I sit down on a big stone in the water and enjoy the nature, the sound of the water, the warm air blowing around my face while I enjoy eating the freshly picked pomegranate. It is a very peaceful moment and once again I feel more like I am on holiday in the mountains than in a war zone.

You can't get enough of moments like this. But the break will be over soon because we still have an appointment with the Governor. During the drive we see more impressive pictures. Here they still work with ploughs pulled by oxen and horses, or the animals are harnessed in front of the wagons, with which the harvest is transported. Finally, we arrive at the Governor's office and during the time when Henning and Nabil are talking to the governor, we are shown the classrooms by a teacher who is responsible for the further education of the governor's employees. He shows us and explains everything that is taught here. From reading and writing in English to computer courses in Word and Excel; and this in a country where there are more illiterate people than people who can actually read and write. This contrast between old traditions and modern equipment is quite extreme. We are also shown old writings and books that tell the history of the province. After the guided tour we will eat together. As usual, the Afghan national dish "Kabili Palau" is served with a lamb skewer and vegetable platter. After the meal we go for a short walk through the village and along the market street. I notice the many small shops where beautiful clothes and fabrics are displayed. The market with its great variety of different spices, of which only some are known to me, really inspires me. What immediately catches my eye is the yellow-golden colour of the saffron, which is available here in large quantities and very cheap. I simply cannot pass by without taking a good supply of it with me. I also have a bouquet of different spices made to send home by post later. Nabil is an enthusiastic hobby cook and knows all the spices for the Afghan dishes by heart, which is why I like to get his advice. I also get some good tips on how to make the spices last longer. "Just freeze it," that's all. After the walk through the city we drive back to Mazar-e Sharif. After about two hours of driving on the Ring Road, we all arrive at the camp healthy and happy from today's trip.

On the way to Samagan, break by the river

Arrival at the town of Aybak

Lunch break for the kitchen staff

Lunch with the Afghan border police

Lamb skewers with flat bread and goat curd cheese and various vegetables

32. The first watch on the watch tower

Like in the last missions, those soldiers who stay in the camp and have no external tasks are assigned to other additional services. In most cases, these additional services are the equivalent to guard duty, which must be provided. Here in the camp, Afghan forces are deployed in the outer area, while soldiers from Mongolia and international comrades are mostly deployed at the main gate. German and Norwegian soldiers are used alternately to occupy the towers around the camp. Since we are mostly on the road during the day, we can only take over the night watch. The first shift lasts from 19 to 24 hours, the second from 0 to 5 hours in the morning. We have decided to take the second night shift. On the day of the night shift, all guard soldiers get a briefing late afternoon from the guard duty officer. He provides you all the information you need to carry out the watch, such as the code word, information on the dress code and the start and end time of the tower watch. We also get the number of the tower we are assigned to. At the end of the briefing you will be subordinated to the guard duty officer for the duration of the tower watch. After being assigned to the watch, everyone can return to their normal duties. Nabil and I meet at the office at about 11:30 p.m. to prepare our equipment for the tower watch and pack them into the car, to ensure a timely arrival at our towers. We have a quick coffee and then head towards our guard shifts. I let Nabil out at his tower and say goodbye to him with the words: "see you later my friend". Afterwards, I drive on to my tower, where I will take over the guard tonight. I park the car next to the tower, put on my 'Bristol', take my P3 pistol and the G36 rifle, my helmet and backpack with rations, and then relieve my comrade from the previous shift.

During the handover process I get a short summary about what has or has not happened in the last hours. After the briefing I quickly call the tower guard to report the handover.

Now I am sitting here and looking down on the illuminated camp and on the airfield, on which some American helicopters are still doing their test flights. It is a somewhat a strange feeling. I am sitting on a chair with a 360 degree panoramic view and I only see a black nothing. But something is moving! I immediately shine my flashlight over to the perimeter fence to see what is going on there. And there it is again!

But it's just a rabbit that is hopping along the fence. However, it is not a well-fed specimen, but a spindly bunny, because the animals generally find little to eat here due to the dry vegetation. It is now 1:45 am and the crickets are chirping. Everything is quiet and with time I start to philosophize about the meaning of life. For the first time I ask myself the questions: What are you doing here? Why are you doing this to yourself? The heat, the faeces dust and the suffering of the people and animals; and also, the mourning for fallen comrades, no matter what nation they belong to. When you stand in line for them and their coffin passes you by, covered with the respective national flag, you always ask yourself these questions, but you quickly repress them and go on with your daily business. Why did so many comrades have to die? The answer is near but also so far away. The intolerance of some people and the lust for power of a few prevent the peaceful coexistence of the whole population. My personal experience with the people here reflects a completely different picture. They too want to live in peace and do their work without fear of death. Although this is only my second tour in Afghanistan, I have returned despite everything. The last time I was in Afghanistan in 2005, I was so impressed by this country and its people that I felt kind of addicted to it. I really wanted to come back here to help the people - no matter how. A second, more personal reason was the separation from my then-wife. Due to the longer professional commitments, this unfortunately happened. This topic is still on my mind now and so the time on the tower passes by.

Two o'clock in the morning. I almost forgot my hourly report to the guard duty officer to whom you have to report every hour. "No incidents", so that the comrades in the guardroom know that you are still alive - in the true sense of the word. Luckily, I managed to send the report in time. Now I have another hour to stare into the nothingness and to let my thoughts wander. However, I always do this with a watchful eye across my allocated area.

The hours go by. It turns 4:05 and suddenly I notice a kind of flash of light on the horizon and then all of a sudden it is as bright as day, as if someone had turned on a light. I have never experienced anything like it. The sun is rising so quickly. At home the sun rises much slower. It takes a good half an hour to get over the horizon so that it is daylight. But here it happens all of a sudden. Less than 30 minutes later the first Tornado Jets are already taking off to take new aerial photographs of the areas they have been assigned to. One can follow them on the runway as they take off and disappear in the bright light of the sun. These are pictures that are otherwise only known from Hollywood movies like "Top Gun".

One more hour, then I will be relieved from my watch. You notice how the whole camp wakes up and slowly the camp life begins. The first sporty comrades run their rounds past the tower and also the first reconnaissance teams with their vehicles leave the camp at the south gate in the direction of Mazar-e Sharif. I can see them all well from my watch post. A new day in Afghanistan begins. It is five o'clock and my relief arrives on time. I pack my equipment and prepare for the handover. My relief is a comrade from the 2nd protection platoon QRF, the Quick Reaction Force, who just returned from a several-day mission two days ago. I carry out the handover with him whilst I also pass on the responsibility for the equipment from the tower to him, like flashlight, field telephone, chair, heating etc.

After five minutes we have completed the handover of the watch. I descend from the tower, put my things into the car and pick up Nabil. Afterwards, we first go for breakfast before we start with our normal duty later. We will catch up on our sleep tonight.

33. Support in driving service for OCCR

Due to our privileges, we as an IEB team can leave the camp at any time of the day or night with our civilian armoured Toyota Land Cruiser. We are not dependent on additional force protection.

This makes it much easier for us to carry out our tasks. Due to this flexibility, we can also easily support other divisions when necessary; so like now the OCCR, whose vehicle is currently broken down. Their service vehicle is a military armoured Jeep, which has the German nickname SSA Wolf. However, it has been around for several years, so it is prone to needing to go to the garage every now and then for a few days to be repaired.

In all collegiality, we offer the OCCR guys that we drive them to their office at 6 o'clock in the morning and pick them up again at 7 o'clock in the evening. That means we can then take the returning shift back with us so that the breakdown of the vehicle does not cause any problems for them.

Thorsten, Klaus, Marc-André and Alex are visibly relieved when they learn that we can take over the driving service. This means for Stephan and me that from now on we will alternate between the early and the late shift, if you can even say that in the field. Here, there are no regular working hours. Every day has 24 hours, and if that's not enough, you'll find extra time somewhere to get the job done.

34. Mr. Scholl-Latour visits Camp Marmal

Anyone, who at one time or another has dealt with the Middle East, must have heard the name Peter Scholl-Latour: the journalist, non-fiction author and publicist has a wealth of experience on this subject like nobody else. Even as a young boy, this man fascinated me because of his open-mindedness and his ability to always get to the heart of the matter. During his studies in 1948, he was already working as a travel journalist for German and French newspapers and radio stations, travelling to many continents from America to Southeast Asia, at a time when I did not even exist. In a few hours, one of the greatest events of my life will take place her in Afghanistan. I will be able to meet this great man personally. This is better than Christmas and Easter put together.

I have heard that Scholl-Latour is on a research trip through Afghanistan for his new book, and that at the age of 87! Respect! And as part of this trip, he will come and visit us for two days. I am sure that he will want to recover a bit from his exhausting journey. There will also be an intercultural evening with insights about the country where we are currently guests. He will be accompanied by a young journalist during this trip. Around 8pm Afghan time, Stephan and I walk from the office towards the Atrium. As we enter, I see Scholl-Latour sitting at one of the tables, where there are even some seats still available. I just look at Stephan and say "Come with me." We walk straight up to the table and ask if we can sit down. To my great pleasure my question is immediately positively answered and so I am able to sit next to one of my great idols.

I take the chair right next to Peter Scholl-Latour and listen to him telling an episode from his life. It is very exciting to listen to him and to hear his experiences personally from him. His story just confirms my own experiences with this country and its people. He talks about the everyday encounters with the Afghan people and their general hospitality in particular. Although he has been to Afghanistan so many times, every visit has been worth the trip, because he can always take new experiences with him from this diverse country, which he then can express impressively in his books.

His new book will again focus on the trouble hot spots of this world. He also briefly discusses the security situation in Afghanistan and tells of the times when it was possible to drive through this country without fear, which, unfortunately, has not been possible in recent years due to the many terrorist attacks.

Peter Scholl-Latour and I sitting together in the Camp Marmal

Listening to him makes me feel like I'm back in the fairytales of a thousand and one nights. Due to his personal experiences, his descriptions are very lively and fascinating. It is not without reason that he has been considered an expert on the Middle East and Islam in the German media for many years. In many debates on television Scholl-Latour he criticized the role of the USA and Great Britain. Based on his great experience, he publicly predicted the long-term failure of the invasions, citing the failure of the Soviet intervention in Afghanistan as one example, among others. Already in the Iranian Revolution of 1979, Scholl-Latour saw the starting point of

a greater "Islamic renewal", which he wrote about in many of his books and which he regarded as one of the great challenges of the new century. Whether in Afghanistan, Pakistan, Syria, Iraq or Iran, those topics were all described and discussed in his books with a lot of suspense and background information. And even now, here in the atrium, one immediately notices that these stories are based on real experiences. Time flies and it is already almost 11 pm when the journalist Scholl-Latour says goodbye and thanks us for the lovely evening. I watch him as he walks away with his travel companion towards the accommodation container. Unfortunately, I cannot attend his lecture tomorrow, because we have an appointment outside the camp. But already these few hours together with this man were just fantastic. For me it was an enrichment to have met him personally and I will always remember this evening with fond memories in the future.

My tour is coming to an end. On October 2, 2010 I will redeploy to Germany and then take leave until the next tour which will not be long. I will also take care of my son, who lives with my wife.

Flight towards home

35. My third mission

I t is the 16th February 2011 and once again I arrive in Cologne Wahn at the Aircraft Operations Department, the so called "Flugbereitschaft" of the Ministry of Defence. In the waiting hall I walk past an information board which read: "Dear passenger! Welcome to the "Flugbereitschaft"! We would like to give you some details about your upcoming flight. Should you have any further questions, please do not hesitate to contact us, we will be glad to help you." Has this notice board always been here? I've flown from Cologne several times, but I've never seen it before. I don't notice the rest of the information on the board anymore, because at that moment I get the smell of fresh Vienna sausages in my nose. And so shortly afterwards I am sitting at the table of the canteen with a lukewarm pair of Vienna sausages with mustard and a bread roll. Almost exactly three months ago I came back from Mazar-e Sharif and now I am sitting here again and it's back to Afghanistan. At that time, it would never have occurred to me at all that I would be back on the flight manifest just three months later. Actually, I had something completely different in mind than going on another mission.

After returning from my last tour, I wanted to start my retraining as a media designer for sound and vision, but this plan was rejected by an employee of the department of employment. Despite all efforts, even whilst in Afghanistan, to achieve a positive result, this man only put obstacles in my way. But as I did not want to register myself as unemployed, I took the opportunity to go on another deployment. Due to my personal engagement,

I got the opportunity to go with the 215 Armoured Artillery Battalion from Augustdorf as a troop supply officer. To this end, I attended a workshop for the introduction of the new computer system "SASPF" in Bremen last week. This is a project of the German Armed Forces for the introduction of standard business software from the SAP AG, a German stock company. At the same time, I also get to meet my new comrades of the department. Since I arrived in Cologne relatively early again, the waiting area is still almost empty. I look around and suddenly I recognize Christian, who has also just bought himself something to eat and drink. I wave to him and he comes straight towards me. I already know Christian from Mazar-e Sharif. He is an IEB officer in Feyzabad and has just returned from leave. He will fly back to Afghanistan with me. The comrades from Augustdorf, who are travelling all together by bus, are still on the way to Cologne.

Slowly the waiting hall of the Aircraft Operations Department is filling up. Most of the people I don't know, because the unit in charge comes from Augustdorf and I have only met a few comrades from there before. But I think that I will recognize several faces during the mission again. Anyway, so far it was always like this. At 12:30 pm the boarding starts, and at 1 pm sharp we take off from Cologne/Bonn towards Termez. But I've also had other experiences in the past. Once, on a return flight in Termez, we waited seven hours because the plane had a faulty system and couldn't take off.

Marcktplatz at camp Feyzabad

36. And back again in Mazar-e Sharif

After a short night in Termez, we landed in Mazar-e Sharif where we are first accommodated in tents at the edge of the runway at the airport, because we are not supposed to fly on to Feyzabad until the next day. At the moment the main phase of the rotation of the troops is in progress. All accommodation containers in the camp, including those for guests, are fully occupied. Therefore, we first have to be accommodated in tents. I hope that we will arrive in Feyzabad the next day as planned.

The next morning after breakfast around 8 am we are standing at the airport and waiting for the plane that will take us to Feyzabad. But after ten minutes my bad premonitions seem to be confirmed. Due to the bad weather conditions in Feyzabad the flight is put off until 11am. At 11am we get the message that the flight has been cancelled completely and that we can return to the tents for the time being. A new departure date has to be arranged. Now we are supposed to fly out tomorrow at 9 am. What can I say? The weather cannot be scheduled and so it is just force majeure that our onward journey is delayed. The problem in Feyzabad is that the runway is located in a canyon and it is a challenge for the pilots even in good weather. In bad weather it is even more difficult; this makes take-off and landing almost impossible. And that is why we are now still stuck here in MES.

New day, new luck, we pack everything up again and off we go to the airport. Luckily, we only have our backpacks with us and don't have to carry our boxes as well. My big box is still at the air transport unit and awaits its onward flight there. The stupid thing is that we have almost no change of clothes in our backpacks, because we didn't expect having to wait here for several days. But we have to take it as it comes. This flight will also be cancelled until further notice. Next appointment: In one week. So now we do not only have a small problem, but already a pretty big one.

In addition, new comrades from Germany are arriving in Afghanistan every day, and the tents are getting very cramped. All of a sudden, we get the information that all those who are supposed to fly on to Feyzabad will move to the squash or sports hall in Camp Marmal, where they should set up their quarters for the next days.

At least we can pick up our luggage in the supply unit opposite the hall. Now I have everything with me again. They distribute laundry bags, so that we can hand in our dirty laundry for washing. Now I realize that our stay in MES will last a bit longer.

We set ourselves up as comfortable as possible in the hall, with camp beds, rubber mats and whatever else is at our disposal. Two streets further up, we can go to the guest shelters for the showers and use all the leisure facilities in the camp. Since I was here only three months ago, I know the camp quite well and we can make full use of all the amenities of camp life; starting with breakfast with the Americans to eating pizza with the Norwegians. At noon a coffee or a Latte Macchiato in the Atrium and in the evening, we went to the OASE for a beer, which was our meeting point for the free time in the camp. After that we went back to our camp beds in the sports hall. That's how we pass our days. As pleasant as they are, it is slowly becoming uncomfortable, as the time for preparing the handover with our predecessors is becoming even shorter. We had not expected such a delay at all. Meanwhile we are stuck here in MES for almost 14 days, and none of us wants to sit around and watch the time pass by. But we have no choice but to wait.

I haven't slept as much in a long time as I have in the last few days; because what else can you do all day long except reading and reading again, or sleeping. I have taken three books with me to pass the time in the evening. But I did not expect that I would read two books in a row in the first 14 days. The first book was written by Marc Lindemann, a former intelligence officer with whom I was on a mission in Kunduz in 2005. The title of the book is "Under Fire. Why Germany is failing in Afghanistan." The second book has a very special meaning for me. When I was in Kunduz in 2005, my mother went to a book presentation from a German Army doctor who had spent many years in Afghanistan. Later that evening after the reading, my mother was so fascinated by this book that she bought it on the spot and also had the author to sign the book with a special dedication. While he was writing the dedication in the book, my mother told him that I was on an assignment in Kunduz at the moment. He looked at my mother and asked, "What's your son's name?" So he wrote on the first page, "To Andreas, with comradely greetings, Reinhard Erös, Colonel Doctor". The title of the book is "Tea with the Devil; as a German military doctor in Afghanistan." I'm actually a notorious non-reader and prefer watching TV or listening to music. But since I was in Afghanistan for the first time, I only read books that have to do with this country; preferably books like this one from the Colonel Doctor.

I absorb one page after the other and very often find his descriptions bring back my own memories. I've come to this beautiful country much later than the Colonel Doctor, but through reading his books it feels like we had been there at the same time. It is the very similar memories that connect me with the author, which also makes this book so special for me. The 16th day in the camp is dawning. Finally, Tino comes to us boys with the more than welcome news. Tomorrow, we are supposed to leave. The Italians will fly us to Feyzabad in a Lockheed C-130. The "Super" Hercules is a turboprop military transporter which can land and take off again in Feyzabad due to its four strong engines. Our Transall with its two engines, on the other hand, would not be able to do this.

Landing in Feyzabad with a Herkules C130

The international airport was built in the 1980s by the Soviet military to transport material, personnel and supplies to Feyzabad.

The runway consists of a 1.8-kilometer-long steel plate construction, which is already in great need of repair. In the event of heavy rain, ice or snowfall, landings in Feyzabad are no longer possible, which has also led to the long waiting time in MES. The airfield is mainly used by the Afghan airline Pamir, the United Nations, international aid organisations, ISAF and various private individuals with their small propeller aircraft like Cessnas. Flight operations are generally carried out according to visual flight rules, since neither beaconing i.e. lighting, nor radio communication exist. A tower for airspace surveillance, a fire brigade, radio and radar facilities, which are required in accordance with international safety standards, are also missing.

37. After 16 days camp stay

Feyzabad (فیض آباد) is the capital of the province of Badakhshan. It is located relatively centrally in the northern half of that province belonging to the Afghan heartland. Our camp is located outside the city, right next to the runway of the capital's airport. The flight with the Italians was fast and good. It is 9:30 a.m. and we have all landed safely, the sun is shining and a cold wind is blowing. On top of the mountains there is still snow shining in the sun. It must have snowed really hard in the last days, because the ground is very soft and partly still very muddy.

The city lies 1,200 meters above sea level and north of the Hindu Kush. A convoy of several vehicles picks us up from the airfield and takes us to the camp. After arriving at the market place, we gather together for our briefing in the "Briefing House". We were only in the camp a for a few minutes, but I can already see that everything here is much smaller and clearer than before in Camp Marmal in MeS. After the briefing we get the keys of our assigned shelters and we can bring our kit to the rooms. Marcel and I will share a room because we will be working in the same department.

The Command Sergeant Major always makes sure that people from the same departments also stay together in their free time. Hence, Marcel and I will share a two-man shelter. The rest of our kit has also already arrived, which is very convenient for me because I can immediately take my travel box with me. Later I'll have a look around the camp. It is always good to know where the important areas are, such as the medical centre, the headquarters, our department, the accounting officer or the cash office and finally the supply department. On the way to the dining room I meet Marcel again and we head for lunch together. We are lucky that here the meals are still prepared by proper military field cooks and not by a catering company. This is also noticeable by the taste of the food. And the kitchen is also more flexible when it comes to changes in manpower within the camp. This is where the former military field cook in me comes out.

As a troop supply officer, however, I no longer have anything directly to do with the kitchen, except for the monthly kitchen committee meetings in which I participate together with my boss, the military doctor and the command sergeant majors of the various companies. But now I enjoy lunch with Marcel first. There is Goulash with pasta and salad, and for dessert a vanilla pudding with raspberry sauce. I can see that not only the German comrades seem to be enjoying the food, but also the Mongolian, the occasional American and Hungarian soldiers, who are also sitting down and eating their meals. After lunch, the obligatory in-processing routine begins. You have to visit a lot of places to get all the things you need for daily life in the camp. Later in the afternoon I have to hand in my medical file in the medical centre. As of now, one of the important tasks is the preparation for the official takeover from my predecessor.

As troop supply officer I am basically the section head of the supply services. But what does this mean? Like during my tour in Kunduz in the 2005, I have to ensure that my subordinated soldiers are able to fulfil their tasks to 100% in their respective areas. This includes operating the filling station as well as the refuelling of both the aircrafts and the large generators that produce the electricity for the entire camp. The first day is coming to an end and I try to process these first impressions whilst lying on my bed. Later my thoughts wander towards home, asking myself what my son Marco might be doing at this moment. He is 6,000 kilometres away from me. He is probably getting himself ready for bed. As soon as I will be able to buy an Afghan SIM card at the local market, I can send my loved ones at home a sign of life from me again.

Magnificent view from the camp

38. The first days in office as troop supply officer

The handover phase with my predecessor worked smoothly. In the next few days the rest of the contingent will have completed the handover phases. Then the first preparations for the implementation of the SASPF programme can begin. Usually, everything that the previous contingent did is in simple terms "crap" and the following contingent is practically reinventing the wheel. But this is not as bad as it sounds. There are areas in which the work was not done as thorough as it should have been. Fuel is one of the areas that our predecessors have not paid so much attention to so far. Here, my boss wants to tighten the so-called belt and intensify the control. The implementation of SASPF, a system that enables us to record all supply items, will force our department to introduce new work processes.

Since we have to enter all the equipment/material that we have, from the living container to the vehicles, generators, weapons, IT equipment and so on into the system, it will take quite a lot of time. In addition, all the daily, weekly, monthly and quarterly reports of the stocks have to be sent to the headquarters in MeS. Then there are all the tasks from my boss which also have to be completed to his satisfaction. Fortunately, every challenge spurs me on a little more to do a good job. And my two comrades in the office support me a lot in this. I could not do it without them, and only as a team we can be strong. I already had this attitude as a young staff sergeant and head of the supply group with responsibility for several comrades and a lot of material of an airborne battalion.

During the time of the contingent change, a lot of handovers occur and everyone who has taken over equipment, be it a vehicle or a complete subunit, like the supply group, has to check it for completeness and functionality, and missing or defective parts have to be recorded. If anything is missing, a property damage report must be written so that the successor has proof of this whenever the next audit takes place. Another task will be to support the Mongolian Guard Company as well as our Force Protection Company with everything that is needed. Therefore, also the air transport unit is an important component of our equipment management, for which I am also jointly responsible.

As I said: there is a lot to do, let's get to work! The biggest challenge we have to face in this contingent is certainly the implementation and operation of the new SAP system for our supply management. And as usual, the teething problems quickly become apparent, which also means that the workload for us will be tripled for the time being. Over time, however, we can correct the errors in cooperation with the IT department, so that the system can run much better afterwards.

39. Support fort he engineer squad

There is always something to do in and around the camp for the engineers. Be it to clear the access road to the camp from the big potholes or to replace broken battens from the runway. And everywhere the AS12B swivel loader, a bucket wheel excavator is used. As I have heard, we also have two of these machines in our camp warehouse. So it occurs to me that I could ask the squad leader of the engineers if I could assist from time to time and thus accumulate sufficient hours to keep my certificate valid. After all, I am trained to operate the AS12B. He gratefully accepts the offer and adds that he will contact me as soon as there is a need. Less than two days later, the squad leader of the engineers calls me to ask if I could support him for a few hours. As usual, the potholes on the access road to the camp have to be filled with gravel again. First I clarify this with my boss. He smiles and just says that I shouldn't get used to doing it all the time so that he would have to do my work for me. I have to grin as well, as he has obviously read my thoughts. Straight after he said this, I am already on my way to the engineers.

Even though I haven't sat on that thing for a few years now, it seems like yesterday that I last drove it; even working with the shovel works. My task today is to fill the truck with gravel and a second Allman distributes the gravel on the road. I am grinning like a little boy playing with his favourite toy. I like this work and it is a lot of fun. After about two hours everything is done and I go back to my office to continue with my actual work.

Two days later my phone is ringing and the squad leader of the engineers is on the line once more and as it sounds, it is now a bigger job waiting for the engineers. The firing range outside the camp is to be renewed and for that all vehicles of the engineers' squad are needed. He suggests that I should drive the big Allman for the project, as he himself will take over the caterpillar and a third man the small Allman. He reckons that the work will take about a total of two to three days. I am happy to say yes again, and later I will try to convince my boss that this mission is very important, not least for the further shooting training of the PRT Feyzabad. Of course I can convince Tino quickly and so I go digging during the day and do my normal work in the evening. Although this is an additional burden, I won't let this fun be taken away from me. The next morning we start. We are leaving the camp together with all the machinery and vehicles in the direction of the old shooting range, which is located directly on a bend of the Kotscha. Kotscha is the name of the river that flows through Feyzabad and which is also used as a swimming pool by the inhabitants of the town; as well as for washing cars. The location of the future shooting range is a real dream. It is situated at the bottom of the water with shooting direction towards a slope. The first thing we have to do is to loosen the ground with the caterpillar and build a mound of earth on either side of the shooting range to ensure that the projectiles cannot cause any damage.

Next, fine sand is distributed over the entire surface so that the cartridges of the different types of ammunition can be collected more easily with a rake. On the second day, the slope is prepared in a way that on the third day we can place the filled sand bags and fill the rest with dirt. The result is impressive. The shooting range is once again in great condition and now we can shoot again. It was three sweaty days of work, but we all really enjoyed it; and I was able to clock up a few hours in my operating log book.

Renewal of the shooting range at the Kotscha

Levelling the shooting range

Since 1986 I have the engineers' certificate for the AS12B Allmann

40. Evening remembrance service for four fallen comrades

It is Thursday morning, more precisely, it is April 15th 2010. The sun is rising and it seems like it is going to be a wonderful day again. I am sitting over a fuel statement to see when we have to order the next tank load of kerosene and diesel to our external storage facility so that we don't fall below the minimum stock level. For this I will use a local Afghan fuel supplier. Around noon I try to call Schoko, our supplier, but the outside line is dead. Whenever something happens, no matter where in this country and German comrades are also involved, a so-called information block is activated. One of the effects of this is that you can only make phone calls inside the camp. As soon as one wants to make an outside call, only the engaged tone is to be heard, as it is now. At the same time the mobile phone network is switched off at short notice. This is to prevent information that has not yet been 100 percent confirmed from leaving the country. When I started to go on missions abroad, I always got confused about this, when I tried to report the error via the telephone helpdesk, until somebody explained it to me how it works. Since then I know that if something bigger happens, the telephone network will be shut down. And then it means waiting until the network is working again. Usually it doesn't take more than an hour for the phone network to be reconnected again, like today. By turning off the telephone network you are warned that something bad must have happened. But what exactly, I will only find out a few hours later.

What I have heard is that there has been an alleged bomb attack. Despite all the bad premonitions and the desperation, even at such a moment the mission must continue and we must not let the insurgents get us down. At least that is what our top leadership and politicians keep preaching. However, after every attack, one is always confronted with the question, why do we actually do this? If one were to be guided only by the bad news, one might think that the operation would be useless anyway. On the other hand, there are situations in which you get the confirmation that it is worthwhile being here. You say "Wow, thank God we're here to help." Like that time in Kunduz when a child lost his whole backside through a Russian mine, but survived because of our medical help.

Finally, late in the afternoon, an information via the intranet comes in that at 7 pm a funeral service for fallen German soldiers will be held in the camp church by our military pastor. After this news we get more and more information about the attack which cost the lives of three of our comrades. During an operation in the Baghlan region they drove their armoured vehicle onto an IED and were killed. A fourth comrade was also killed in the subsequent fire fight with the insurgents whilst trying to provide assistance to the injured comrades. With this news I get a strange feeling in my stomach.

In the region where the incident happened, I drove through with our Toyota a year before and I remember a beautiful area with large, extensive fruit plantations, and now this! Somehow the pictures from back then don't really want to fit in with the events of today. Back in the present: Tino, my boss, is sitting in his office, which is directly opposite us. We communicate with each other in an uncomplicated way through the open doors. When he wants something from me, he usually comes over and then distributes the orders. But now he calls me over and tells me that we will all attend the field service together after dinner and that I should inform the other two comrades. I nod in agreement and go back to my place. After dinner we go directly from the mess hall over to the field church. On the way there, more and more comrades from other departments join us and when we open the door of the field church, it is almost completely filled. We sit down on the remaining free seats in the second from last row. On the altar there are three pictures in frames with the fallen comrades, a burning candle and a cross. I am sitting on my wooden chair and take a closer look at the photos of the fallen comrades. And I am thinking "Oh, man, thank God it's not you whose picture is on that altar." In moments like this, you realize how much you care about your life. Although I am normally not the faithful believer, in this moment I think of him and thank him that I am doing so well. The evening prayer for our fallen comrades is accompanied by a very appealing story from our military chaplain Stephan, and the Lord's Prayer still works like it did in religious education. After the evening prayer there is a final drink at the chaplain's house; after that I go to sleep.

Pastor S. at the evening service for the fallen soldiers

41. The blue heart of Feyzabad

Since February 2011, the rescue centre of the PRT Feyzabad has been responsible for admitting German and Afghan patients. A comrade, whom I only got to know and appreciate here during my tour, is André. He is a chief petty officer, a so called "sprat" from the north of Germany. André, with the nickname "Richy", loves his job as a soldier and medic; you can see that immediately. We met here in Feyzabad in the medical centre when I handed in my health file on my arrival. We got on well right from the start. The main task of the Feyzabad Rescue Centre is to take care of the German soldiers. If there is free capacity, treatments are also carried out on Afghan patients. The most common ailments the medical team here in Afghanistan has to deal with are burns, scalding with hot water and traffic accidents; but also tumours, infections, bullet and splinter injuries. Richy goes out on patrol and organizes the daily routine at the rescue centre. In the morning he personally picks up the Afghan patients at the main gate and accompanies them to the field hospital. This reminds me of a nice experience.

One morning, the head of the supply unit and I are walking towards the main gate to take over a "Jungle Truck" that was loaded with a bulldozer. I accompanied the driver to the unloading point and watched Richy talking to an Afghan man at the gate with the help of his interpreter. The man was probably the father of a little girl who was hit by a car and suffered severe leg injuries. That's why she had to regularly visit the PRT for follow-up examinations. The six-year-old girl was lying on a stretcher and on the way to the ambulance she suddenly started to cry. She was probably scared and still in a lot of pain. Richy saw the girl crying and immedi-ately took her in his arms. As soon as she was in Richy's arms, everything was fine again. He carried her to the ambulance, which then drove her to the medical centre. Her father was watching Richy with his daughter and had to smile. He put his right hand over his heart and just said "Taschakor" - Thank you. That moment sent shivers down my spine – although it was more than 40 degrees outside. I found it quite extraordinary. But with such small and inconspicuous acts and the gratitude we experienced, one is reminded again that our efforts are worth wile: "Because we are here to help". The same evening, I also find out the name of the little girl. Her name is Zora. Because of his helpfulness, most patients call Richy only "yek ghalbe abi baraye Feyzabad" - the blue heart of Feyzabad. This name is a sign of great gratitude, because the expression refers to the blue gem-stone lapis lazuli, which is very important for the Af-ghans. So it is a very fitting award for Richy.

Finally, Richy also inspired me to get a dog. He showed me pictures of his little dog on his mobile phone and how they romped around on the beach together. And what can I say? I finally could not resist. Eight months later these pictures were the reason why I got my own dog again. A black Labrador Retriever named Lucky.

And that`s Lucky today at the age of 9

Richy, a great comrade and friend

A precious smile

189

42. Lunch with „Schoko"

We've been working here in Afghanistan for three months now, and I have to say that things are going better than we thought. The SASPF system is now being used diligently and otherwise the normal madness prevails. Every day everyone tries to do everything humanly possible to support the comrades who are doing their job outside the camp as best as they can. The generators have to run all the time and without fuel this is of course not possible. As far as the supply of fuel is concerned, we are, so to speak "at the back of beyond" and completely dependent on our suppliers, unlike our comrades in Mazar-e Sharif or Kunduz. That is why we should continue to maintain the good relationship we have had for years with Abdul Halim Schokrulah, nicknamed "Schoko". Therefore, one of my first duties when taking over the business from my predecessor was to introduce myself to Schoko.

When I first met Schoko, I knew right away that I would be able to work well with this man. We immediately had a good connection to each other, because Schoko could speak and understand the German language very well. He lived in Germany for several years and worked there in the catering business in different places. When he returned to Afghanistan, he and his brother founded their current company with the headquarters being in MES and a branch office in Feyzabad. Once a week, his trucks drive to MES and back to get the fuel we need. Since the current contracts with Schoko have to be renegotiated in the near future, I suggest that we visit him soon to inspect his fuel depot. That way we will be able to see how much fuel Schoko

190

can actually store. This information is important for us, because in the winter time the journey to MES and back can take several days due to the bad road conditions and the snow-covered passes. All this information will later be included in the negotiations. To visit Schoko, we take the car and drive in the direction of the airport and turn onto the main road towards Isari, a small village at the edge of the airport. Schoko's premises are situated at the outermost area of the airport, where both its fuel depot and its residential house are located; the latter in the middle of a beautifully landscaped garden. Since not everyone is allowed to drive outside the camp, I ask Christian, our IEB officer, if he would accompany us to Schoko, because he has a so-called "Green Card", which gives him permission to leave the camp at any time of the day or night. Christian was immediately enthusiastic about the suggestion to visit Schoko. I made an appointment for the four of us with Schoko for 12 o'clock. Since it is not too far away, Florian, André, Christian and I meet at the car shortly before 12 o'clock and start our little trip. A few minutes later we already arrive at Schoko's yard. We haven't even turned off the engine yet, when he comes towards us with his youngest grandson in his arms.

A warm welcome with hugs follows as is customary in Afghanistan. After that, Schoko shows us his small but fine refinery as well as his fuel trucks and his beautifully laid out property with the house. You can already see from the furnishings that Schoko is better off than most of the other Afghans. But like in Germany, you have to work hard for success and here and for Schoko it is no different. After the tour we will have lunch with Schoko's whole family. The Afghan hospitality is reflected not only through their warm and courteous manner, but also in the generous and delicious food. All for the benefit of the guest. From the starter to dessert, different creations of food are always served in large quantities to cater for every taste and to make sure that everyone is satisfied. A single dish is therefore rather seldom the case and it does not matter what living circumstances the guest or host come from. As a guest, one should politely eat everything and have at least one second helping, because only satisfied guests make the host happy. Of course I do not want to be responsible that our host feels insulted, and so I try my best to be a good guest. We take a seat on his veranda with real Afghan carpets and large cushions. Like on most occasions when guests are expected, the Afghan national dish is served. Traditionally, Afghans eat on the floor. The meal is spread out on a cloth, called "Distarkhan", and the guests take a seat around it. The food is eaten with the fingers of the right hand. The rice dishes Chalau and Palau, Qorma, stew, similar to Indian curries, kebab, various salads, pickled vegetables, yoghurt and fresh flat bread are part of every meal. Dookh, a refreshing yoghurt-cucumber-mint drink, is often offered as a drink with the meals. The dessert then consists of black or green Chai, sweet pastries, various puddings, the "Firni", pulses, dried fruits and plenty of fresh fruit. All these delicacies are now also served to us from Schoko. In addition, he offers us homemade lemonade which is really good in this heat. In such moments, being well fed, one can really lean back and let go for a short time. Christian and I look at each other and have the same thought: nap. That would be a fine thing now, but duty calls and we unfortunately have to say goodbye to Schoko and his family and drive back to the camp.

Schoko and his pride and joy:
his cockrel

Schoko`s tank farm and one of its trucks in Feyzabad

43. A reunion with Nabil, Sultan, Soraya

I n normal life, it often happens that you don't see each other for years after school or apprenticeship, until the first class reunion when you are over the age of 30. In the German Army it can happen that you haven't seen each other for years, and then you meet again on a mission. That's how it was for me in MES in 2010, when I met my former company commander again after 13 years. During this tour I also met another comrade with whom I was stationed in Kunduz in 2005. They also say that the Army is like one big family, you meet again and again, be it on training courses or on a mission. It's just before noon and I'm having lunch with Marcel, when Nabil enters the mess hall. What a surprise, I thought to myself when I saw him. I didn't expect to see him again so soon. I jump up and run towards him. We hug each other and are both completely flabbergasted that we are already on duty together again; not in the same department, but in the same camp after all. What I'm most interested in is in which department he is in and for how long he will stay here in Afghanistan. This time he is only deployed as a interpreter. Nabil actually wanted to work in the IEB area again, but this position was already filled. I ask him if he has heard anything from Sultan and Soraya and how they are doing. Nabil smiles and says that Sultan will come to Feyzabad in the next few days and Soraya works in MES as the personal interpreter for the commander, i.e. for the Major General. She has already announced that we will have visitors in the near future. Nabil and I spend the whole lunch break talking about our last mission together. We had a good time there, despite some dark days when we lost comrades. I remember the beautiful trips with Heike and Soraya to the women's shelters, to the children's home and to the orphanages. We had so much fun and Soraya was totally absorbed in this task and her eyes were shining like stars in the night. Back then, whenever I visited Soraya in her interpreter's office, there was always a good green tea and pistachios to nibble on.

In the evening I meet Nabil at the bus stop in the camp again and we are sitting together on the bench. It has already become very dark and the stars are shining in the sky. Like me, Nabil looks up into the sky and with a somewhat sorrowful sigh he asks why it can't always be as peaceful in this world as it is at this moment. I agree with him and suggest that we go to bed with this thought and hope that there will be many more such peaceful and beautiful evenings here in Feyzabad and in this world.

A few days later, Sultan arrives in Feyzabad. The first time we see each other again is in front of the headquarters, whilst I am on my camp tour. I don't even notice him at first, because I'm lost in my thoughts about work again and rummaging around in my files. But suddenly I hear someone calling my name. I turn around and Sultan is standing there in front of me. I am overjoyed to see him, but unfortunately, I cannot talk to him for long, because I still have a lot to do. So I suggest to Sultan that we meet sometime for a coffee or tea, which he agrees to with a broad grin, and then I continue with my camp tour. Because I had a lot of work to do, it still took a few days for us to meet for a tea. But then, I am pleased to see that Sultan is still the same: in a good mood and always up for a joke.

44. Attack on German armed forces in Takhar province

T oday, the Major General together with Sultan's sister Soraya will pay us a visit. I'm still sitting in my office and working on some property damage reports before I want to go on my morning round through the camp again. I usually have the door of my office container open, so that I can see more than just my little four walls. That's why I can immediately hear the helicopters approaching. Most of the time, they fly above us to the landing site. Suddenly, Nabil is standing in front of the door and announces that Soraya has landed with the general. I look and wink at him with a smile on my face.

I was just about to head off and do my camp round anyway. When I pass by the market, Soraya runs right into my arms. We are so happy to see each other again, but unfortunately, she only has a little time, so we can only have a short talk. To say goodbye, I give her a big hug and wish her good luck and success in her work. She quickly runs towards the headquarters and I, a little slower, towards the supply unit. As she disappears around the corner, I once again think back to the time we spent together in MES with a smile on my face. Today runs smoothly and seems to end just as nice as it started, but suddenly, at 9 pm, everything changes. I'm still sitting in the office when I overhear some comrades talking outside. They were saying that one comrade was killed in an IED attack in the province of Kunduz. These are the moments when you reflect and start a conversation with the good Lord, asking Him to hold His hand over you for protection. The next morning, however, routine has already caught up with us again. It is the 28th of May and I start my working day like every morning with a rich breakfast together with Marcel.

Unfortunately, with time one becomes immune towards bad news about death. There isn't a day that goes by in which a soldier doesn't die in Afghanistan. Our therapy is very simple; we talk about it over dinner. Despite the constant threat and uncertainty in this country, a day in the field cannot begin better than with a good breakfast.

And again, the phones are dead around noon. I find out exactly what happened when I read the following news-flash on the intranet: "Explosive attack on the governor's palace in Taloqan. At the time of the explosion, high-ranking delegations from Germany and Afghanistan were staying there; several dead and many seriously in-jured." At this point, I don't know who was killed and who was "only" seriously injured. But what I do know is that Soraya and the General are there!

I'm trying to reach Nabil, but I can't get him on the phone. At this moment, everything is going through ones head but nothing positive. I know that Sultan is out and will not return to the camp until later. It is already after 11 p.m. and I am still working in the office, when I hear soft voices from outside. I jump up and run outside the office. Nabil and two other translators are standing and looking at each other silently and very sadly. No one says anything anymore, and only their eyes speak volumes. Without thinking I ask the question I don't want to raise. "Is she dead?" Nabil, of course, under-stands immediately and shakes his head. Fortunately, the worst misfortune had not occurred, but Soraya is said to be among the most seriously wounded, but no details are known as yet, except that she is being operated on at the field hospital in Mazar-e Sharif.

At this moment, Sultan arrives. He gets out of the car and walks straight towards us. I look him in the eyes and take him firmly in my arms. "It's going to be all right. She is in good hands and she is a fighter. She's gonna make it!" As I am saying the words to Sultan, I notice that tears are running down my cheeks. Somehow, it is only now that I realize what has happened. We all try to calm Sultan down and to help him, but it is not that easy. Our leadership is making every effort to organize a helicopter to take Sultan to MES. The only problem is that it is already quite late and the helicopters do not fly in the dark. I learn the next morning that Sultan was picked up very early and that he is already with his sister in MES. , Nobody in the camp knows yet how Soraya is doing. It is being said that she is in a "critical condition" - and that can mean anything. I have barricaded myself in my office and pray to God that he will accompany her on her difficult journey and not give up on her. On this morning, after the cruel attack, no one can really understand how close death can come to you here again and again. Even if attacks occur in the south of the country, you repress this thought so as not to drive yourself crazy. After all, the tasks have to be carried out in spite of everything that happens. So there is nothing I can do, but hope with all my heart that a miracle will happen and that Soraya will survive and be completely healed.

Saluting soldiers at a mourning ceremony for the fallen comrades

45. Father`s Day run at Camp Feyzabad

The preparations for the 2011 Father's Day Run are in full swing. This year, Father's Day falls on the second of June, which is next Thursday. Therefore, the elements of the engineers are already preparing parts of the ring road for this. The ring road runs inside the outer perimeter fence and completely surrounds the entire camp. Three stations for food and drinks will be set up. There will be containers which will be filled with cold water by the camp fire brigade in the morning before the run to cool down the water bottles and cold drinks for the runners.

I am a father myself, but on this day, I will take care of the many runners together with the support staff and not take part in the run myself. Apart from that I am not a great runner, but prefer mountain biking. But Tino and Marcel, my department mates, are taking part in the run. They have already made internal bets about who will be the best at the end. It's nice to watch a major and a sergeant major competing with each other for the award of the best runner in the J4 department. In order to get fit for the day, the two of them will from now on throw themselves into their sports gear in the evening and run their laps diligently. Many departments of the contingent, including those of other nations, are registering teams for this run, including the Operational Mentoring and Liaison Team, OMLT, of which I know one lieutenant well. These guys support the ANA soldiers who have set up camp right next to our accommodation. They do weapon training with the soldiers, show them how to detect and disarm booby traps, but also how to set up and operate a checkpoint properly.

During one's tour, one gets to know many new comrades from different units and areas, as I did with my comrades from the OMLT. All of them have to come to us when they need something. After all, that's what we are here for.

Back to our Father's Day run. You can run 15, 20 or 25 kilometres, depending on what everyone wants to run. I don't know exactly which route my two mates will take, but I believe I'm not so wrong in thinking the 20 kilometres. Since our colleagues from the fire department often go to play beach volleyball, I thought that it would be a great additional training for Tino and Marcel to play a round with them. So I ask Tino and Marcel if they would like join in for a match! The ground couldn't be nicer either, with fine sand from Afghanistan. No sooner said than done. So I organise a match to play with - or against - the colleagues from the fire department. But what they don't know yet is that the appointment will be at 5pm this afternoon; two days before the Father's Day run.

Their enthusiasm is limited and only a reserved and a not very keen O.K. come out of their mouths. I myself have never played beach volleyball until today and I am curious to see what will happen. I know that it is very sweaty and exhausting, but that's sport for you. Around 5 p.m. the three of us and another comrade from the HQ staff are at the playing field and are already warming up until the colleagues from the fire department arrive. It is fun to jump around barefoot in the still hot sand like a stork and to dive after the ball so that it doesn't touch the ground. A short time later the lads from the fire department appear. So now we can form two teams and start the actual game. After only a few minutes of fast rallies, adventurous dives and crashing hits, we all realize enthusiastically that from now on we want to meet regularly every Wednesday evening to play, at least as far as the duty schedule allows. After two hours of intensive volleyball play, which we unfortunately lose by two sets to five, we say goodbye to the lads of the fire department with the words: "See you next Wednesday for revenge!"

Freshly showered and with a full stomach after the evening meal, a little while later, I am lying relaxed on my bed. I can already feel the strain in my muscles and say to Marcel that I couldn't possibly run 15 kilometres the next day. Fortunately, I only have to serve drinks. Marcel just laughs and notices that probably Tino will struggle tomorrow too. I am grinning at this thought and then read a bit in my book before I fall asleep.

As the saying goes, "The early bird catches the worm". It's four o'clock in the morning, the marshals and support staff meet at 4:50 a.m. to coordinate the final arrangements for the Father's Day run. The first runners will start at 5:30 am. This is just a precaution to ensure that the last runners do not have to finish their run in the midday heat. Luckily the sky is a bit cloudier today, so the temperatures are not that high.

Normally, on a sunny day, we already have up to 29 / 30 degrees Celsius around 7 am. I go out with a comrade from the fire department to fill the containers with water and set up the umbrellas and tables at the refreshment stations. Besides the drinks, there will also be orange and banana pieces for the runners. We are assigned to the second station outside of the camp and we are waiting for it to finally start. In the distance we hear the starting signal punctually at 5:30 am and the announcement over the radio that the first runners have started. After a few minutes they already pass our refreshment point for the first time. None of the runners wants to have anything yet, but that will change quickly as soon as the sun comes out and it gets really warm. I pay close attention to whom is passing by, because I want to cheer Tino and Marcel on - and of course the others too.

On the 2.5 kilometre lap the guys pass by us more often. Marcel and Tino are doing well, both are in the midfield. But soon, as the saying goes, "the chaff separates from the wheat", which can be seen at every marathon run. Lap after lap the effort is more and more written in the boys' faces, and the drink cups we handed them are also gratefully accepted. The sun above us is burning down relentlessly. My respect for the running comrades increases with every round. I am really glad that I only have to serve them the cool drinks and not to have to run along myself. Around 10 o'clock the last runners reach the finish line. Relieved and exhausted, but happy to have put the exertions behind them. It was a lot of fun to watch the guys running and cheering them on. Now it's time to clean up and later we'll go to the volleyball court for the award ceremony.

At the award ceremony my two favourites unfortunately don't get a trophy but only a certificate. But that doesn't matter, because everyone had fun anyway. Each of the participants and the helpers will receive a T-shirt with the inscription "Father's Day Run Feyzabad 2011". We end the day having a barbecue together, which, of course, includes a Father's Day beer as an ultimate highlight.

Although it is slightly cloudy, the guys are starting to sweat

46. Departure

Our time in Feyzabad is slowly coming to an end. Actually, our replacements should have arrived already, but the weather has once again put a damper on our plans. Not even our transport planes can take off at the moment; that's how bad it is. We feel like we are sitting on hot charcoal and would like to hand over our duties.

I can see it coming again, that we'll only be able to leave here at the last minute and then, in worst case, we might have to wait in Termez for spare parts for the plane back home, just like last time. Well, we'll see how it goes. Today is Schoko day again. Our reliable supplier delivers diesel for our fuel deposit tanks. The winter is approaching fast, and so we should have enough fuel available in store. Therefore, I will also stop by the fuel deposit tanks later during my tour through the camp and say "hello" to Schoko.

Anyway, I still have to exchange a few words with him regarding the required quantities and the provision over the winter months. Throughout the whole camp one can sense the imminent change of contingent. As with any other contingent, losses and damage to material are detected through the audit controls, and brought back into balance by a damage report or a repair order. Although it is the same procedure every six months, you never get it timed so that everything is 100% complete by the time you hand it over.

But we'll try our best to make it work better this time. My guys from the Supply, the Fuel and the Ammunition Groups, and finally the Clothing Chamber have been checking their area for a few days now and taking an inventory at the same time. Although I only got to know them shortly before the mission, I always find that my comrades from Augustdorf are simply unbeatable when it comes to readiness for action, working ethos, and the implementation of orders and assignments. I have never had such good people under me in the field and I would like to take this opportunity to thank all my comrades once again for their constant loyalty.

Not to forget of course my two mates, Tino and Marcel, who also did a great job, especially in the early days with the changeover to the new SASPF system and the takeover from our predecessors. None of this would have worked if our boss Tino hadn't had our backs and kicked us "in the butt", when needed. Also, to him I would like to say many thanks and appreciation for this wonderful time.

I really hope that we will meet again soon after the mission and that we will not lose contact with each other. But enough of that; Schoko is probably already waiting for me together with Florian.

Pictures that I will never forget; impressive and beautiful at the same time

„You feel like yor`re in another world"

47. Back home

It is Friday, October 21, since two days I am back from my mission and private person again. The return from Afghanistan was like always, except that this time I swore to myself to stop smoking as soon as I set foot on German soil.

I have tried it several times before, but it hasn't worked so far. This time, I was ready for it and wanted to see it through. That is one of my strengths. When I really put my mind to something, I can do it. The first two days passed quickly, without me even touching a single cigarette. And I have been able to stick to it until now.

On Monday, 24 October, my retraining as a media designer for image and sound will begin in Stuttgart. I am curious to see what will happen. I will definitely be the oldest in the class, which is not too bad.

But first of all, I have given myself a gift that I have been dreaming of for a long time. I had already established contact to a breeder of Labrador retrievers from Afghanistan. He has a new litter of puppies since August 8th. I will visit this breeder at the weekend to see which of the little puppies fits best to me. I am already looking forward to having a dog again. There will be a lot of work to do at the beginning, but I am sure that I will manage it. In any case, it will be worth the effort, because a dog like this at your side outweighs all the work with his loyalty.

Last week, still in Feyzabad, I phoned Sultan and found out that Soraya, in the meantime, was staying in the army hospital in Koblenz. She still has some operations ahead of her, but from a medical point of view she is over the worst of it. When I heard that, I was very relieved and thought that things can only get better for her now. I met with Nabil before I left. We agreed that we would meet sometime in the next few weeks. He lives in Karlsruhe and that is not so far away from where I live.

My family is happy that I returned home safe and sound. My son Marco jumped into my arms and gave me a firm hug and said "Good to have you back". I couldn't really show my feelings at that moment, but inside me it was like a volcano erupting. I had missed him very much, which became even clearer to me now that I held him in my arms again. But when you are in a foreign country for so long and every day you have so many positive, but also negative experiences, it always takes a few days or even weeks until you get used to life at home again. Changing your daily routine and finding your way around in the family, whether it is shopping or simply setting the table for dinner, these are no longer familiar tasks as they were before the assignment. You feel naked and exposed without the safety of the gun holster on your thigh. Wearing jeans, T-shirt and sneakers has become something unusual. They are light as a feather compared to the weight of the desert camouflage uniform with the combat boots. During the mission, larger crowds of people were generally avoided in daily life, so that now the normal weekly market in the town or the Saturday shopping tour through Stuttgart's Königstrasse no longer have anything relaxing about them, but rather represent threatening situations. One would prefer to stay at home, lock oneself in a room and not let anyone come near one. But anyone who has been on a mission abroad knows that this is not the way to do it.

That's why I'm going to plunge right back into the hustle and bustle and take the crowded tram to Stuttgart every day to start my retraining measures there. Humans are creatures of habit and that's why they quickly get used to new circumstances again. And I make use of that. My retraining as a media designer for vision and sound has been going on for almost four weeks now and I am actually the oldest in the class. But I don't mind that at all. I was even elected "class representative". Back then, during my time at school, it would never have occurred to me to even let myself be nominated, but here I have great fun doing it. Next Friday afternoon, I will be going with my son Marco and Maike, a girl of his age from the neighbourhood, to pick up our new family member Lucky, a male Labrador. It will be a new era in our lifes with such a little animal at our side.

There is a lot going on at the moment and I don't even have time to think about the last mission in Afghanistan. In school, every now and then, I tell a few episodes from life there, because in my class there are some soldiers who are doing their civilian vocational training. And because I need a clear head for new input at the moment, I postpone the reflection to a later time. I plan to write a book about all my missions in Afghanistan, so that every reader who knows a little about the German Army can understand how life is in an operational area - without being influenced by the media.

48. Eqilogue

To summarize I can say that the time in Afghanistan was, despite the pain and suffering, a very beautiful time as well, that I would not want to miss. It definitely changed me. This experience will accompany me throughout my whole life. I hope that through this book I have been able to give many people, young and old, an insight into the culture and life in Afghanistan, so that they can now better understand why the Germany Armed Forces is defending the domestic peace at the Hindu Kush. Unfortunately, many comrades, Germans, but also from other nations, lost their lives there. In my opinion, the way for a peaceful Afghanistan could have been paved as early as 2005 through more specific actions by ISAF troops. Unfortunately, the moment was missed when it would have been possible to eliminate the then still small factions.

After returning from the mission, a so-called "returnee seminar" was offered for the comrades, which unfortunately I could not attend myself. In these seminars, the impressions and events during the mission are discussed and processed. Unfortunately, there are far too many comrades who come back with post-traumatic stress disorder, the so-called PTSD. I, on the other hand, immediately threw myself back into everyday life again at home and now I am processing my experiences through this book. With some of my comrades from the time of my missions I still have a lively and friendly contact. Nabil, for instance, is still a very good friend who, among other things, helped me with his excellent skills as a translator, to convert the place and common names in this book into the national language Dari.

The social networks have also proved to be very beneficial for me to keep in touch with my friends Marco and Sultan. In this way I also regularly find out from Sultan how Soraya is doing and I always send her my regards. I have also developed a close friendship with Tino, my last boss in Feyzabad, and we talk on the phone regularly. Since his mission in Afghanistan, among other things, he went on a tour as a NATO observer in Mali, Africa. I have also established a very good contact with my former boss, Colonel Baur, since we first met in Mazar-e Sharif in 2010. In the meantime, he has left the German Armed Forces and is enjoying his retirement. I also still have a regular exchange with Brigadier General R. I think it is nice to continue to hear from the people who mean a lot to you as friends and comrades. I was especially happy when I heard great news from the US artist Batuz a few weeks ago. Among other things, he used the experiences in Afghanistan and from our joint project to realize his dream of his own museum, so that he can communicate his message of peace between people better. Privately, a lot has changed for me as well. I have been living alone in my own apartment for over a year.

In the meantime, I'm divorced. Lucky, my dog, is already four and a half years old. We are a good team and we both volunteer in a rescue dog group as a certified rescue team. In the meantime, Marco is a 22-year-old man who has the same hobby as his father had when he was twenty: helping to work the fields with all kinds of tractors. Now we get along very well, which was not so easy at the beginning after the separation and me moving out. I can understand him, and he also understands now why I took this step. That is why we try to make the time that we spend together enjoyable and fun - which of course is not always easy.

My son Marco and I, driving a tractor

49. Attachment 1 Rank groups from army

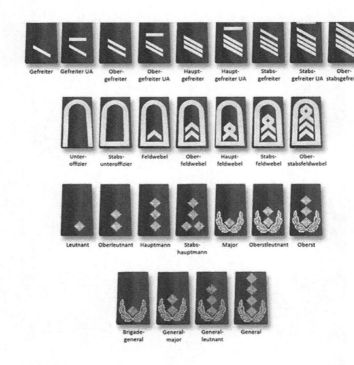

50. Attachment 2 Mongolian ranks

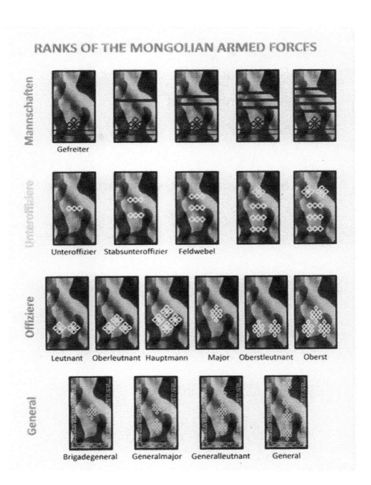

RANKS OF THE MONGOLIAN ARMED FORCES

Mannschaften

Gefreiter

Unteroffiziere

Unteroffizier Stabsunteroffizier Feldwebel

Offiziere

Leutnant Oberleutnant Hauptmann Major Oberstleutnant Oberst

General

Brigadegeneral Generalmajor Generalleutnant General

51. Attachment 3 Breakdown of a guide

- S1 – staff
- S2 – position management
- S3 – commitment
- S4 – care
- S5 – public relation
- S6 – Information/communication (IT)
- S7 – care, support

52. Attachment 4 Classification of NATO classes

Fuel, Otto- (for cars)	F-46/F-50
Fuel, diesel- (for cars)	F-54
Fuel, Otto- (for Aircraft)	F-12/F-18
	F-22
Fuel, turbines - (for Airkraft)	F-34/F-35
Fuel, turbines - (for Airkraft)	F-40
Fuel, turbines - (for Airkraft)	F-44
Ethanol denatured	S-738
Pure methanol	S-747
petroleum	F-58

53. Attachment 4 Translation from German to Dari

Personen / peopel

Atta Noor (Gouverneur von Balkh)	عطا محمد نور
Herr Batuz	باتوتس
Hadji Atiqullah Ansari	حاجى عتيق اللهانصارى
Hadji Hayatula Direktor für Hadj	حاجى عيات الله
Hadji Zalmai (Stammesoberhaupt)	حاجى زلمى
Wasiq	وثيق

Städte / Cities

Aliabad	على آباد
Aybak	اىبک
Baghlan	بغلان
Balkh (Provinz)	ولايت بلخ
Bamian (Provinz)	ولايت باميان.
Bagdad (Hauptstadt Irak)	بغداد
Feyzabad	فيض آباد
Hairatan	حيرتان
Herat	هرات
Islamabad	اسلام آباد
Kabul	کابل
Kandahar	کندهار

Kunduz	کندوز
Mazar-e Sharif	مز شریف
Pol-e Khomri	پل خمری
Takhar(Provinz)	ولایت تخار
Taloqan	تالقان
TermezUspekistan	ترمز/ اوزبیکیستان
Samangan	سمنگان
Sar-e Pul	سرپل

Nahrungsmittel / food

Feigen	انجیر
Fladenbrot	نان خشک
Granatapfel	آنار
Grüntee	چای سبز
Honigmelonen	خربوزه
Lammfleisch	گوشت گوسفن
Pistazien	پسته
Quabili Palau Nationalgericht	قابلی پلو
Paprika / Peppers	مرچ دولمه
Rosinen / raisins	کشمش

Sonstiges / miscellaneous

Kokcha (Fluss in Feyzabad)	دریای کوکچه
Taschakor	تشکر

54. Attachment 5 in alphabetic order

ABP	„Afghan Border Police"
ANA	Afghan National Armee
ANP	Afghan National Police
ANSF	Afghan National Security Forces, trained by NATO
AVZ	Foreign usage surcharge § 56 Federal Salary Act for soldiers participating in humanitarian missions abroad
Booby traps	A Booby Traps is a device or setup that is intended to kill, harm, or surprise a person or animal
BRISTOL	Bulletproof vest
BesAnLog	Special instruction logistices different methods of material management
BMVg	Federal Ministry of Defense
CIMIC	Civil Military Cooperation

„Dress-code"	Describes rules and regulations for the desired clothing in the country of use depending on the risk situation.
EOD	„ Ordnance disposal"
EPA	One man pack Food package for a soldier for a daily ration
EVG	Individual consumer goods are replenishments that are subject to wear and tear, but are only delivered to the front when required or in small quantities.
ESGA	Basic training for deployment Afghanistan
HQ-RC-N	Headquarters of the Regional Command North
ISAF	International Security and Assistance Force International securithy and support forces or protection forces.
IEB	Intercultural mission advisor (advising commanders abroad)

IED	„improvised explosive device", unconventional explosive and fire devices
Kaleu	Lieutenant rank for naval uniforms
LUZ	Air handling train is responsible for all material that enters and leaves the country.
MVG	Bulk goods are goods that are consumed and required by the troops in large quantities. This primarily includes ammunition, fuel and food.
NVG	Non- consumer goods are goods that are normally not subject to consumption, such as vehicles,etc.
OCCR	Operation Coordination Center Regional
OMLT	Operational Mentoring and Liaison Team trains Afgan soldiers according to German infantry principles.

OvWa	Security officer, means the position of the train driver of a military or civil guard train.
Portepee	The non- commissioned officers with Portepee from a rank group of the Bundeswehr (German Arme)
PsyOps	„Psychological Operations" „Psychological Warfare "
PSO	Peace Support Operations military and civillan measures to prevent conflict and ensure peace.
QRF	„Quick Reaction Force" Rapid intervention as an operational reserve for the commander.
RDL	Reserve service Providers
RPG	Rocket Propelled Grenade Anti-tank grenade.
RPSE	Regional PsyOps Support Element
Suicide	Suicide bomber

SASPF	A project of the German Arme to introduce standard business software from SAP AG
TAA	„Target Audience Analysis" Target group analysis.
TVB	Troop supply worker is responsible for the logistics of the camp.
TAC-P	Tactical Air Control Party (Tactical air force control personnel have the task of requesting aircraft and instructing them at their destination).
Gating	Temporary subordination of one or more soldiers to a supervisor during guard duty. In civil life,zhe term is also used colloquially for instruction.
ZENTRA	Central troop training for deployment in Kosovo and Afghanistan.
ZAW	Cicilian training and further education measure.

55. Attachment 6 List of figures

Page 14   Map of Afganistan

               (source wold at las)

Page 22   sunset in the camp

               (source A.Meyer)

Page 28   Afgan security forces at work

               (source A.Meyer)

Page 29   flight to termez with the CH53

               (source A.Meyer)

Page 37   Grief in the first hours

               (source A.Meyer)

Page 42   waiting for material from Germany

               (source A.Meyer)

Page 44   flight with CH 53 to Feyzabad

               (source A.Meyer)

Page 46   Austrian soldiers on patrol

               (source A.Meyer)

Page 48   spice market in Kunduz

               (source A.Meyer)

Page 49   Street vendor of flatbread in Kunduz

               (source A.Meyer)

Page 54   entrance to the emergency

                 (source A.Meyer)

Page 54   A jungle truck brings material

                 (source A.Meyer)

Page 56   Heavy earthquake in northem Paki-
                 stan 2005 (source US Air Frorces)

Page 61   mourning party for Achim who fell in
                 Kabul (source German Army)

Page 63   waiting at the finish in the French Pau
                 (source A.Meyer)

Page 65   This time again with the helicopter

                 (source A.Meyer)

Page 68   the gate to Termez (source A.Meyer)

Page 71   view from the dining room to the liv-
                 ing container (source A.Meyer)

Page 75   With this C160 he flew away

                 (source A.Meyer)

Page 79   At home, such pictures are no longer
                 visible (source A.Meyer)

Page 83   Sadly, I had to see this picture way to
                 oftem (source German Army)

Page 89   Getting to know Governor Atta Noor
                 in person (source A.Meyer)

Page 93   Visit at the children`s home in Mazar
             e Sharif (source A.Meyer)

Page 93   They like to be photographed with us
             (source A.Meyer)

Page 94   Heike is surrounded by Afgan youth
             (source A.Meyer)

Page 94   The slightly different one drives a car
             (source A.Meyer)

Page 97   Visiting Colonel B. in camp Spann
             (source A.Meyer)

Page 99   Entrance to the Blue Mosque
             (source A.Meyer)

Page 102   The front yard of the Blue Mosque
             (source A.Meyer)

Page 107   Students leaving the Teacher
             Training Center (source A.Meyer)

Page 109   Taking care of the drivers
             (source A.Meyer)

Page 110   Election candidate Jawid Barrad
             (source A.Meyer)

Page 110   Afgan food,traditionally eaten with-
             out cutlery (source A.Meyer)

Page 113   Stephan and Nabil, my teammates at IEB (source A.Meyer)

Page 119   Fotoshoot on the roof of the Markentender (source A.Meyer)

Page 120   A visit at Radio Andernach

(source A.Meyer)

Page 120   SatCom Sergant working

Page 121   Nabil playing kicker at Radio Andernach in the camp (source A.Meyer)

Page 126   at the gate by Nabil and me

(source A.Meyer)

Page 132   Helmets for Peace, courtesy of artist Batuz (source A.Meyer)

Page 133   Preparation for day X with Hungarian support (source A.Meyer)

Page 134   tow CH53 flying low over the camp

(source A.Meyer)

Page 139   Batuz a man who can enchant people (source A.Meyer)

Page 139   Breaking bread as a symbol of how enemies can become friends (source A.Meyer)

Page 140   Friendly embrace (source A.Meyer)

Page 140   Implementation of the human chain with Afgan staff and soldiers of all nations (source German Army)

Page 144   Uzbekistan border crossing to Afghanistan Hairatan (source A.Meyer)

Page 144   "Welcome to Afghanistan"

(source A.Meyer)

Page 149   Marc-Andrè is aleays up for a joke

(source A.Meyer)

Page 149   Alex,not only a comrade, but a good friend (source A.Meyer)

Page 152   On the way to Samagan, break by the river (source A.Meyer)

Page 153   Arrival at the town of Aybak

(source A.Meyer)

Page 153   Lunch break for the kitchen staff

(source A.Meyer)

Page 154   Lunch with the Afghan border police

(source A.Meyer)

Page 154   Lamb skewers with flat bread and goat curd cheese and various vegetables (source A.Meyer)

Page 162   Peter Scholl-Latour and I sitting together in the Camp Marmal (source A.Meyer)

Page 164   Fligt towards home

(source A.Meyer)

Page 167   Marckplatz at Camp Feyzabad

            (source A.Meyer)

Page 171   Landing in Feyzabad with a Herkules
            C130 (source A.Meyer)

Page 175   Magnificent view from the camp

            (source A.Meyer)

Page 180   Renewal of the shooting range at the
            Kotscha (source A.Meyer)

Page 181   Levelling the shooting range

            (source A.Meyer)

Page 181   Since 1986 I have the engineer`s cer-
            tificate for the AS12B Allmann
            (source A.Meyer)

Page 185   Pastor S. at the evening service for the
            fallen soldiers (source A.Meyer)

Page 188   And that`s Lucky today at the age of
            9 (source A.Meyer)

Page 189   Richy, a great comrade and friend

            (source A.Meyer)

Page 189   A precious smile (source A.Meyer)

Page 193   Schoko and his pride and joy: his
            cockrel (source A.Meyer)

Page 193   Schoko`s tank farm and one of its trucks in Feyzabad (source A.Meyer)

Page 198   The Governor`s building after the attack (source A.Meyer)

Page 199   Saluting soldiers at a mourning ceremony for the fallen comrades (source A.Meyer)

Page 204   Although it is slightly cloudy, the guys are starting to sweat (source A.Meyer)

Page 206   Pictures that I will never forget; impressive and beautiful at the same time (source A.Meyer)

Page 207   "You feel like yor`re in another world" (source A.Meyer)

Page 213   My son Marco and I, driving a tractor (source A.Meyer)

Page 232   Images that will never leave your head " beautiful" (source A.Meyer)

Page 233   A look into the " unknown"

            (source A.Meyer)

Page 234   Girls in a girls`school in the tent

            (source A.Meyer)

Page 235   Sand storm in Feyzabad

            (source A.Meyer)

Page 236 „Children in another world, but thankful that they live" (source A.Meyer)

Images that will never leave your head "beautiful"

A look into the „ unknown"

Girls in a girls`school in the tent

Sand storm in Feyzabad

„Children in another world, but thankful that they live

Lightning Source UK Ltd.
Milton Keynes UK
UKHW020605080223
416671UK00001B/71